Analyzing Children's Play Dialogues

Frank Kessel, Artin Göncü, *Editors*

NEW DIRECTIONS FOR CHILD DEVELOPMENT
WILLIAM DAMON, *Editor-in-Chief*

Number 25, September 1984

Paperback sourcebooks in
The Jossey-Bass Social and Behavioral Sciences Series

Jossey-Bass Inc., Publishers
San Francisco • Washington • London

Frank Kessel, Artin Göncü (Eds.).
Analyzing Children's Play Dialogues.
New Directions for Child Development, no. 25.
San Francisco: Jossey-Bass, 1984.

New Directions for Child Development Series
William Damon, *Editor-in-Chief*

Copyright © 1984 by Jossey-Bass Inc., Publishers
and
Jossey-Bass Limited

Copyright under International, Pan American, and Universal
Copyright Conventions. All rights reserved. No part of
this issue may be reproduced in any form—except for brief
quotation (not to exceed 500 words) in a review or professional
work—without permission in writing from the publishers.

New Directions for Child Development (publication number
USPS 494-090) is published quarterly by Jossey-Bass Inc., Publishers.
Second-class postage rates are paid at San Francisco, California,
and at additional mailing offices.

Correspondence:
Subscriptions, single-issue orders, change of address notices, undelivered
copies, and other correspondence should be sent to Subscriptions,
Jossey-Bass Inc., Publishers, 433 California Street, San Francisco
California 94104.

Editorial correspondence should be sent to the Editor-in-Chief,
William Damon, Department of Psychology, Clark University,
Worcester, Massachusetts 01610.

Library of Congress Catalogue Card Number LC 84-80837
International Standard Serial Number ISSN 0195-2269
International Standard Book Number ISBN 87589-985-4

Cover art by Willi Baum
Manufactured in the United States of America

Ordering Information

BF
717
.A54
1984
c.1

The paperback sourcebooks listed below are published quarterly and can be ordered either by subscription or single-copy.

Subscriptions cost $35.00 per year for institutions, agencies, and libraries. Individuals can subscribe at the special rate of $25.00 per year *if payment is by personal check*. (Note that the full rate of $35.00 applies if payment is by institutional check, even if the subscription is designated for an individual.) Standing orders are accepted. Subscriptions normally begin with the first of the four sourcebooks in the current publication year of the series. When ordering, please indicate if you prefer your subscription to begin with the first issue of the *coming* year.

Single copies are available at $8.95 when payment accompanies order, and *all single-copy orders under $25.00 must include payment*. (California, New Jersey, New York, and Washington, D.C., residents please include appropriate sales tax.) For billed orders, cost per copy is $8.95 plus postage and handling. (Prices subject to change without notice.)

Bulk orders (ten or more copies) of any individual sourcebook are available at the following discounted prices: 10-49 copies, $8.05 each; 50-100 copies, $7.15 each; over 100 copies, *inquire*. Sales tax and postage and handling charges apply as for single copy orders.

To ensure correct and prompt delivery, all orders must give either the *name of an individual* or an *official purchase order number*. Please submit your order as follows:

Subscriptions: specify series and year subscription is to begin.
Single Copies: specify sourcebook code (such as, CD8) and first two words of title.

Mail orders for United States and Possessions, Latin America, Canada, Japan, Australia, and New Zealand to:
  Jossey-Bass Inc., Publishers
  433 California Street
  San Francisco, California 94104

Mail orders for all other parts of the world to:
  Jossey-Bass Limited
  28 Banner Street
  London EC1Y 8QE

New Directions for Child Development Series
William Damon, *Editor-in-Chief*

CD1 *Social Cognition,* William Damon
CD2 *Moral Development,* William Damon
CD3 *Early Symbolization,* Howard Gardner, Dennie Wolf
CD4 *Social Interaction and Communication During Infancy,* Ina C. Uzgiris
CD5 *Intellectual Development Beyond Childhood,* Deanna Kuhn
CD6 *Fact, Fiction, and Fantasy in Childhood,* Ellen Winner, Howard Gardner

CD7 *Clinical-Developmental Psychology,* Robert L. Selman, Regina Yando
CD8 *Anthropological Perspectives on Child Development,* Charles M. Super, Sara Harkness
CD9 *Children's Play,* Kenneth H. Rubin
CD10 *Children's Memory,* Marion Perlmutter
CD11 *Developmental Perspectives on Child Maltreatment,* Ross Rizley, Dante Cicchetti
CD12 *Cognitive Development,* Kurt W. Fischer
CD13 *Viewing Children Through Television,* Hope Kelly, Howard Gardner
CD14 *Childrens' Conceptions of Health, Illness, and Bodily Functions,* Roger Bibace, Mary E. Walsh
CD15 *Children's Conceptions of Spatial Relationships,* Robert Cohen
CD16 *Emotional Development,* Dante Cicchetti, Petra Hesse
CD17 *Developmental Approaches to Giftedness and Creativity,* David Henry Feldman
CD18 *Children's Planning Strategies,* David Forbes, Mark T. Greenberg
CD19 *Children and Divorce,* Lawrence A. Kurdek
CD20 *Child Development and International Development: Research-Policy Interfaces,* Daniel A. Wagner
CD21 *Levels and Transitions in Children's Development,* Kurt W. Fischer
CD22 *Adolescent Development in the Family,* Harold D. Grotevant, Catherine R. Cooper
CD23 *Children's Learning in the "Zone of Proximal Development,"* Barbara Rogoff, James V. Wertsch
CD24 *Children in Families Under Stress,* Anna-Beth Doyle, Dolores Gold, Debbie S. Moscowitz

Contents

Editors' Notes 1
Frank Kessel, Artin Göncü

Chapter 1. Children's Play: A Contextual-Functional Perspective 5
Artin Göncü, Frank Kessel
A dynamic analysis of play dialogue emphasizes and illustrates the ways in which play and players evolve.

Chapter 2. The Organization of Dramatic Content in Children's Fantasy Play 23
David Forbes, Gary Yablick
Presenting a structural view of fantasy conversations, this chapter describes dramatic elements of play that reflect developing social knowledge.

Chapter 3. Text and Context: Fabling in a Relationship 37
Diana Kelly-Byrne
A phenomenological account of play interaction locates the construction of meaning within the historical context of the players' relationship.

Chapter 4. Text and Context in Imaginative Play and the Social Sciences 53
Brian Sutton-Smith
Understanding the social and cultural contexts of play requires appreciation of both natural and interpretive science and appraisal of their views of symbolic behavior.

Chapter 5. New Wine in Old Bottles 71
Greta Fein
Four primary problem areas that arise in the discussion of text and context can best be addressed in a natural science framework.

Chapter 6. Annotated Bibliography 85
Artin Göncü, Frank Kessel

Index 91

Editors' Notes

Using children's dialogues in play as a paradigmatic case, the chapters in this volume explore varied meanings of the notions of *text* and *context* and consider their potential significance for child development and its study. The overall purpose of such exploration and consideration—undertaken in varying blends of the conceptual and the empirical—is threefold: to shed light on some substantive aspects of children's imaginative play and play dialogues, to view some other dimensions of child development in that light, and to stimulate discussion of different modes of developmental thought and research. As such, this volume provides grist for the mental mills of students of development whose primary interest lies in communication, in play, and in facets of cognitive, language, and social development. But, more significantly, in presenting an initial exploration of text and context in play dialogues along empirical, theoretical, and philosophical lines, the chapters will—we hope—constructively serve those seeking to cut across what have become conventional categories of development.

Since the cast and character of the volume reflect its origins, we should note that early versions of the chapters were presented as part of a symposium at the 1983 Annual Meeting of the American Educational Research Association (AERA) in Montreal. Although the primary focus of that symposium was on imaginative play per se, it was our judgment that the notions of text and context might have wider import, especially when viewed within the framework of communication or dialogue, and, further, that some fundamental conceptual and methodological issues could be discerned in the not-too-distant background. Fortunate enough to have William Damon accept that judgment and to receive his generous encouragement, we proceeded with a moderate degree of reframing of those AERA symposium presentations for the present volume. (Judith Van Hoorn's paper on infant games, while not included here, was a valued part of the symposium.)

Since imaginative play is still clearly in focus it will be apparent why we refer to the reframing of the original symposium papers as

1

moderate. But the picture presented by the volume has a number of further, interrelated dimensions: The notions of text and context are considered in terms beyond play; an array of ideas on the function and structure of dialogues between child and child and between adult and child are explored; and the nature and merits of interpretive science and natural science approaches are examined.

It is here that these chapters reflect features of a still wider scene. For, as developmental psychology searches for its post-Piagetian identity, a variety of conceptual and theoretical accounts of the relation between the developing individual and the social world are being explored: script theory (Nelson, 1981), action theory (Meacham, 1984), and Vygotskyan theory (Wertsch, 1984). And as psychology and the social sciences in general acknowledge the postpositivist temper of the times, alternative philosophical traditions and research approaches are being scrutinized: hermeneutics and phenomenology (Rorty, 1979), ethnography and ethnomethodology (Geertz, 1983), and literary theory (Mink, 1981). In touching on such general topics and themes, this volume might, therefore, make a modest contribution to the kinds of conversations Kessen (1983) has called for in the study of child development:

> We can only celebrate the end of the era of positivistic psychology as manifest destiny and applaud the new, more modest recognition of our limitations and of the cultural complexity of the child. But to preserve child psychology..., certainly to see the child in society, we must be able to talk across the boundaries of the special empirical domains. Somehow the new experts and their students have to be able to talk to one another. Those conversations, it seems to me, must take place in two forms. And these are the new visions of developmental psychology that I see. The first conversation is... within the nation of child psychology if you like, speaking across the special domains of the field itself.... And the other conversation we need is the conversation among people who have worked in different disciplinary areas, along the national boundaries of our special fields.... If we were truly to recognize that the study of children is not exclusively or even mainly a scientific enterprise in the narrow sense, but stretches out toward philosophy and history and demography, if we were to recognize such an expanded definition of child study, we might anticipate a new form of

investigator, a new "scientist" in Dewey's terms, whose object of study is not the true child or my piece of the true child but the changing diversity of children [pp. 38-39].

Frank Kessel
Artin Göncü
Editors

References

Geertz, C. *Local Knowledge: Further Essays in Interpretive Anthropology.* New York: Basic Books, 1983.
Kessen, W. "The Child and Other Cultural Inventions." In F. S. Kessel and A. W. Siegel (Eds.), *The Child and Other Cultural Inventions.* New York: Praeger, 1983.
Meacham, J. A. "The Social Basis of Action." *Human Development,* 1984, in press.
Mink, L. O. "Narrative Form as a Cognitive Instrument." In R. H. Canary and H. Kozicki (Eds.), *The Writing of History.* Madison: University of Wisconsin Press, 1981.
Nelson, K. "Social Cognition in a Script Framework. In J. H. Flavell and L. Ross (Eds.), *Social Cognitive Development: Frontiers and Possible Futures.* Cambridge, England: Cambridge University Press, 1981.
Rorty, R. *Philosophy and the Mirror of Nature.* Princeton, N.J.: Princeton University Press, 1979.
Wertsch, J. V. *Cognitive Developmental Theory: A Vygotskyan Approach.* Cambridge, Mass.: Harvard University Press, 1984.

Naturally no conversation-in-print is ever possible without the person who, at a touch, can turn text into type. For making this volume possible we extend sincere thanks to two such persons—Debbie Comeaux and Tracy Owens.

Frank Kessel is associate professor of psychology at the University of Houston. He received his Ph.D. from the University of Minnesota in 1969 and is coeditor of and contributor to The Child and Other Cultural Inventions.

Artin Göncü is a research associate at the Center for Advancement of Child Care and Education and a lead teacher at the Human Development Laboratory, University of Houston. He received his Ph.D. from the University of Houston in 1983.

Children construct and organize their knowledge of the social and physical world in dyadic play in an increasingly reciprocal way.

Children's Play: A Contextual-Functional Perspective

Artin Göncü
Frank Kessel

Developmental psychology has witnessed a burgeoning interest in the study of imaginative play during the last decade (Fein, 1981). There have been numerous efforts to identify the kinds, components, correlates, and developmental consequences of play (Rubin and others, 1983). A variety of topics and issues have characterized these efforts. Play transformations (viewed as expressions of symbolic development), the relationship between imaginative play and other aspects of cognitive development (such as language and divergent thinking), and the training of children in play have been three of the areas subject to

We are indebted to several people for allowing us to conduct this study in the University of Houston's Human Development Laboratory: Carol Quarton, former director, Rheta DeVries, present director, and Joan Sheldon, assistant director. Special thanks are extended to Ruth Dickey and Rama Ramanadhan, lead teachers, and all the children for their happy cooperation.

research scrutiny. Discussion has been focused on how much emphasis should be given to imaginative play activities in preschool curricula in order to foster development of both social and cognitive skills. Answers have been sought to questions such as whether play is primarily an assimilatory activity, as Piaget (1962) proposed, whether it is an essential mechanism in the development of language, as Vygotsky maintained (1978), and whether play is linked to autonomous and flexible psychological functioning (Sutton-Smith, 1983).

The nature of play and its role in development have been explored from different theoretical viewpoints. Given the richness and diversity of play, various conceptualizations can be, and have been, proffered. For example, Sutton-Smith (1980) noted that Erikson has focused on autonomy as revealed in play, Berlyne emphasized arousal modulation in play, and Bateson conceptualized play as a form of communication, while Piaget viewed play as an expression of symbolic representation. Despite these different types of conceptualizations, however, contemporary developmental studies have presented a principally cognitive picture of play. Inspired to a large extent by Piaget (1962), a host of studies were conducted over the past decade to determine the course of symbolic development as expressed in various transformation modes such as decontextualization, self-other relations, and sequential combinations (Fein, 1981). Researchers (for example, Elder and Pederson, 1978; Pederson and others, 1981) influenced by Vygotsky (1978) have also viewed play mainly as a tranformational activity and have directed their attention to the substitution of objects.

Several features of research in the past decade on imaginative play are worth noting: First, the majority of these studies have been experimental in nature rather than observational (for example, Jackowitz and Watson, 1980), while such studies have tended to take place in laboratories rather than naturalistic settings (for example, Fein, 1975). Second, the various kinds of transformations have largely been analyzed separately and in static terms (for example, McLoyd, 1980). Third, as Rubin and others (1983) observed, solitary rather than social play has commanded the greatest attention. As a corollary to the second and third features, little is known about how children interact with each other during social imaginative play (Field and others, 1982; McLoyd, 1980), or about how they communicate with one another regarding their transformations (Fein and others, 1982).

In more general terms, neither the existing studies of solitary play nor those of social imaginative play have explored in any detail how the context for symbolic representations is dynamically or functionally created and expressed. How do children become engaged with one another in imaginative play and, once engaged, how do they understand and relate to each other's imaginative constructions? How do they reach consensus, if they do, on the representation of reality in play? How, in summary terms, do children initiate, maintain, and terminate play? In our view, full understanding of play and its role in development will require answers to these kinds of questions.

Against this background, the present report is a product of a study (Göncü, 1983) that concerned itself with both symbolic representations in children's play and the processes involved in creating interpersonal frameworks for such representations. An attempt was made to develop a contextual-functional view of play by linking cognitive (Piaget, 1962) and communicative (Bateson, 1955) theories and borrowing concepts from speech act theory and methods from discourse analysis (Bruner, 1974/75). With much of the discussion of cognitive and communicative considerations presented elsewhere (Göncü and Kessel, 1983), the present chapter will focus on and begin to explicate the functional nature of play dialogues. We will do so by outlining two approaches to children's dialogues, one metacommunicational and one conversational, laying out a few basic notions of context as part of the first outline. In each of these sections, we will present the coding scheme used in the Göncü study (1983), also illustrating how a play dialogue can be analyzed in terms of these approaches. After reviewing some specific findings, we will end with a discussion of them and of more general issues.

Play-as-Communication

According to Bateson (1955), the most distinctive feature of play context is that it is metacommunicative. In his seminal work, Bateson states that "play could only occur if the participant organisms are capable of some degree of communication, that is, exchanging signals which would carry the message 'this is play'" (1955, p. 3). Bateson refers to the conveying of this general message and of more content-related ideas about play as "framing." Through such framing, actions and utterances in play are interpreted at a representational level rather than at face value. For Bateson, a metacommunicative utterance—such as the explicit statement "This is play"—conveys the message that "those actions in which we now engage do not denote what these actions for which they stand would denote" (p. 3). For example, a child pretends to have a phone conversation with an imaginary grandmother and then asks her friend, "You know what? Our grandmother is gonna come over here and have a great big party at my house, right?" Here, she is making a statement which refers to an imaginary state of affairs and, seen in context, is also inviting her friend to participate in planning for a party. In this view, then, in order for social imaginative play to begin and continue, partners must be informed about the change from non-play to play and about the nature of play activity.

Several theorists and researchers have begun to build upon Bateson's point of view. At a conceptual level, Sutton-Smith (1983) suggests that establishing play context involves the players orienting themselves and others to meaning and to the potentially varied and complex levels of meaning in their activity. An immediate implication of this view is that children bring some ideas to their play and then work toward a consensus about what will constitute a shared symbolization of objects, identities, and situations. As a corollary, to a greater or lesser degree, and more or less explicitly, children will negotiate with one another to resolve interpretive discrepancies.

The general view of play as communication, therefore, calls for an examination of such interactions, a step undertaken in at least two previous studies. In an ethnographic study of kindergarten children's interactions in a variety of contexts, both in and out of play, Schwartzman (1978) demonstrated how the broad social setting influenced children's play and its themes. In particular, she found that metacommunicative statements reflected children's inclination to exercise control or, more generally, their ongoing relationships. Thus, the metacommunicative messages of a dominant child, as established through independent observations and sociometric measures, were different in nature from the messages of less dominant children. It is this system of ongoing relationships that Schwartzman considers the most important aspect of context.

In another ethnographically-oriented study, Garvey and Berndt (1977) explored how three-, four-, and five-year-old children create contexts for their imaginative play. Defining context at a more specific level than Schwartzman — as action formats or plans which influence the kind and nature of transformations — Garvey and Berndt identified forms of communication between pairs of children. Their results indicated, first, that dyads at each of the age levels were more likely to give metacommunicative messages, such as plans, than to make symbolic transformations. Second, in all cases, plans were more likely to refer to the child's own activity than to their partner's or the dyad's. Also, the oldest children were more likely than the other two groups to mention their partner's role. In general, noting the high frequency of explicit messages and how transformations are embedded in the context of announced plans, Garvey and Berndt (1977) draw the following conclusion:

> The point to be made about the communication of pretending is that a good deal of talk is directed to creating, clarifying, maintaining, or negotiating the social pretend experience. In order to pretend you must know who your partner is, what he thinks he is doing or intends to do, where he thinks he is, and what it is he is handling or using; he must have similar information about you. Further, since children of this age probably do not talk silently to themselves (Conrad, 1971), it is likely that by verbalizing their transformations they also assist and support themselves in pretending. To some extent, then, the saying *is* the playing at this age [p. 7].

The Present Study: Classifying Play Utterances

Within the framework of the concept of play as communication and these studies by Schwartzman (1978) and Garvey and Berndt (1977), one aspect of our research has focused on how three- and four-and-a-half-year-old preschool children familiar with one another create, in dialogue, contexts for their imaginative play texts. A detailed description of the category system devised for classifying play utterances can be found in Göncü and Kessel (1983). Here we present only a brief summary of the categories and results in order to provide some background for our principal concern in this chapter.

- *Invitations.* Statements that are explicit requests for play are coded as invitations (for example, "Let's play with the blocks"; "Do you wanna play with me?").
- *Plans.* These are statements which express the orientation of self, of partners, or both (self and partner) toward current and ensuing activities (for example, "You're gonna cook"; "We're gonna dance and marry").
- *Object statements.* These statements indicate possession of play materials. They also specify whether objects belong to self, partner, or both (for example, "This is our truck"; "Those are my flowers").
- *Transformations.* Statements which exhibit a quality of nonliterality are coded as transformations. They are expressions

of the ways in which imagined identities, objects, and situations are represented (for example, "This pipe is my gun"; "We're now at the restaurant"; "I am the mother now").
- *Acceptance statements.* These give explicit approval or acceptance to announced transformations (for example, "Isn't it sad that a sea-monster came and broke it?" *"Yeah"*).
- *Negations.* Statements that are explicit refusal or rejections of announced transformations are coded as negations (for example, "I am Superman." *"No, you aren't, you are small."*).
- *Termination statements.* Statements which signal or announce the end of an activity or episode or the end of play itself are coded as terminations (for example, "I am not gonna play with those blocks anymore").

Our analysis, based on the distribution of seven kinds of metacommunicative statements across two ages and sexes, revealed significant results only for the distribution of statement types. The statements were not equally likely to occur. Sixty-five percent took the form of transformations, plans and object statements constituted 12 percent and 13 percent respectively, while the remaining forms were infrequent (invitations, 2 percent; acceptance statements, 3 percent; negations, 4 percent; terminations, 1 percent). These findings, which hold at both age levels, suggest that most metacommunicative statements in social imaginative play are expressions of symbolic representations rather than comments and negotiations about such representation. The preschoolers in this study consistently made few explicit invitation and termination statements; that is, they move in and out of play episodes largely implicitly. Similarly, they seldom explicitly accept or reject their play partner's transformations. In general, then, we have a picture of dyadic play in which there is a great deal of consensus between the partners on their representation of reality.

The implication of these findings for Bateson's view of play as communication is discussed in Göncü and Kessel (1983). Here, we note that although this sort of analysis of metacommunicative statements sheds light on how much talk is devoted to various forms of framing and symbolic representations, it does not yield direct information on whether, and how, coherence and continuity are established in play conversation. For example, although we know that the preschoolers agreed on what and how to play—as indicated by the large proportion of transformations and plans—we do not know how such statements are connected in the course of play. Therefore, we have moved on to examine, in a preliminary fashion, how the preschoolers' utterances are dynamically and functionally related to each other in the flow of their play dialogues.

Play-as-Conversation

The second dimension of our research that bears on the present discussion aims to develop an analysis of the conversational function of the kinds of metacommunicative statements listed above. Such metacommunicative taxonomies do not directly address the questions of how children respond to each other's declared and implied expectations, intentions, and needs. In our view, a dynamic analysis of play dialogue should take into consideration both how continuity is established in conversation and whether certain metacommunicative statements are more responsible than others for the continuity and coherence of dialogues. In this way, not only will we obtain information about how children expand their conversations, but we will also gain knowledge of how children relate to each other's evolving imaginative worlds.

Consider the following example: As two boys of the same age are playing together, one of them puts a piece of material over his shoulders and announces, "I am Superman, I have a cape on." The other, taller child appears dissatisfied with his partner's idea, pulls the "cape," and responds, "No you aren't, you're short." From a metacommunicative point of view the children are said to be negotiating, with the first child's identity transformation being negated by the second. Thus, coding in terms of metacommunicative categories tells us that there is one transformation and one negation statement in this interaction. Such coding does not, however, convey much about the dynamic, functional properties of the conversational exchange. If we were to consider the second child's intentions, we would be able to determine how he negates his partner's transformation by adding a new dimension to the ongoing conversation.

The process by which children come to maintain continuity and coherence in conversation has recently begun to come under scrutiny in developmental psycho- and sociolinguistics (Brown, 1980). With play dialogues in mind we turned to some of this literature. Bruner (1974/75), for example, borrows from speech act theory in exploring how children's expression and interpretation of intentions emerge in the course of early interactions with an adult (usually the mother). Prior to speech the intention to communicate is first expressed in the form of innately determined behaviors such as crying. At a later point in infancy, once the child's attention has been secured, it is sustained in what Bruner terms *joint action formats,* the development of these formats presenting a predictable pattern (in games or routines such as Peek-a-Boo). Although the infant initially enters and engages in such interactions only as a demanding partner, with age he or she becomes able to engage in reciprocal interactions which involve the setting of boundaries and the division of labor in "conversation." The expression and interpretation of intentionality in joint action formats are thus relative to both the present activity and the partners' expectations of each other based on the history of their prior interactions.

Consistent with Bruner's proposals, descriptions of prelinguistic and early linguistic communication between children and adults indicate that adults initially take the primary responsibility of interpreting intentions and organizing the interactions. Kaye and Charney (1980), for example, have described the communicational asymmetry between twenty-six- and thirty-month-old children and their mothers. Studying the conversational status of play-turns, Kaye and Charney found that mothers of children in both age groups took an active role in interpreting their children's messages, in expanding the conversation, and in keeping the topic intact. Similarly, Dore (1979) showed that while three-year-olds in preschool settings engage in task-related exchanges with one another, such interactions are structured, controlled, and supervised by their teachers.

Although these studies illuminate the role of adults in bringing children to the point of jointly contributing to ongoing conversations, there is less evidence on how children maintain conversations with one another (Ervin-Tripp and Mitchell-Kernan, 1977). More to the present point, we know of little work on the development and dynamics of dialogues in play. There are, however, two studies that form the immediate background for the present investigation.

Garvey (1974), in another report based on the play of three-, four-, and five-year-olds, identified the function of turns and noted that they fall into two major types—the child either repeats what the partner has said or complements his or her partner's utterance. According to Garvey, doing or saying the same thing as the partner may imply acknowledging the partner's intentions. Doing or saying a complementary thing, however, implies accurate interpretation of the previous speaker's intent and of his or her act's function in the interaction. For example, when one of our four-and-a-half-year-old girls told her partner, "Wait, before we go to bed we have to eat and dance," her play partner responded, "Yeah, well, we need to clean up all this stuff, too." Here, the second child both agrees with her friend that they will have fun before they go to bed and she adds that the house must also be cleaned. Garvey, based on her qualitative analyses of dialogues, concludes that the older children in her sample were more likely to complement their partners, while younger children mostly repeated their partners' utterances or actions.

In a second study of direct relevance here, Torrance and Olson (1982) proposed a scheme for classifying conversational function which complements Garvey's observations. These researchers examined, in a preliminary fashion, how children establish continuity and coherence in conversation by specifying the degree of relevancy between the turns taken by game partners. Categorizing conversational turns as either turnabouts, responses, or mands (see below), Torrance and Olson found that children from four to six years old become more effective in establishing explicit connections between their partners' turns and their own.

The Present Study:
Maintaining Imaginative Play Conversations

Based on the work of Kaye and Charney (1980), Garvey (1974) and Torrance and Olson (1982), we have sought to examine how children maintain their imaginative play conversations. Below is the category scheme we have used for analyzing the functional value of play utterances.

- *Turnabouts.* These are utterances that provide a response to the expectancy and intention established by the previous speaker and add a new expectancy which maintains the conversation. In this sense, turnabouts not only establish a relationship between what had been said by the partner and what the child is saying but also prepare the ground for the partner to then respond further. Therefore, a turnabout is the most cohesive discourse device in this classification (for example, "I'm Superman." *"No, you aren't, you're short."*).
- *Responses.* Simple acknowledgements or refusals of the intentions or expectancies established by the previous speaker are coded as responses (for example, "Isn't it sad that a sea-monster came and broke it?" *"Yeah"*).
- *Mands.* These are utterances that establish a new expectancy without making direct reference to the previous speaker's utterance but also without changing the topic completely (for example, "What are those hats for?" *"I am wearing the funny hat"*).

- *Unlinked Utterances.* Utterances that are in no way relevant or connected with the previous speaker's are coded as unlinked (for example, "This car has a telephone." "*I made pancakes.*").

An Illustration. Consider now the following exchange between two four-and-a-half-year-old girls as an example of how conversational function of metacommunicative statements can be determined:

R and *A* are in the dress-up corner of the play room. *R* wears a ballet tutu and holds a bouquet of flowers. *A* wears adult size shoes, carries a purse and tries to put on a tie. Having observed *A* dress up, *R* takes the floor.

R: 1. We're in this room and nobody can squeeze through this room, only a mouse. (Holds flowers and extends arms, showing *A* the room.)
A: 2. That's right. (Stands at the clothes rack holding a tie.)
R: 3. *A*, I'm going to a wedding.   4. I have to call the wedding man. (Appears amused.)   5. Who is going to marry me? (Smiles, puts hand on waist moving her hips in a dancing fashion.)
A: 6. Nobody is going to marry you, you're just on a dance! (Very stern, places tie on the rack as she talks to *R*.)
R: 7. We are going to dance with flowers, aren't we *A?* (Gestures with hand, appears enthusiastic.)
A: 8. Me and you are going to dance. (Walks over to the phone.)
R: 9. I have to phone call 'cause I'm going to marry. (Picks up the receiver.)
A: 10. You have to... (Picks up a broom, motions with broom.)   11. You have to phone call, tell who you're gonna dance with.   12. And then you are going to go there.   13. And then we're gonna give him his wife.   14. And then we're gonna tell him all about who we're gonna marry.   15. And then he'll say okay.   16. And then we can go stand on the steps on the stage and dance.   17. It is really a big stage.
R: 18. Yeah, it's really.

After *R*'s response, *A* starts sweeping the floor with the broom. Stops. Puts the broom on the shelf and tries to smell *R*'s flowers.

A: 19. Let me smell the flowers *R* (Approaches flowers.)
R: 20. No, no. Don't pick them anymore. (Pushes *A*, protecting flowers with hands.)

The girls have a brief conversation on flowers and this episode of "marriage-and-dance" ends.

The episode begins with *R* announcing in an unlinked utterance her plan of going to a wedding (3). Having indicated what she would like to do (4), *R* enacts role of a young woman who will be getting married, that is, *R* transforms her identity (5). This transformation, however, is not totally accepted by *A*, who expands the topic in a negation statement which is also a turnabout (6). *R*'s following utterance, a joint plan, is also a turnabout since she not only responds but also announces an intention of dancing with flowers (7). *A* then rephrases this joint plan via a response that reiterates what the action format is (8). At this point, the flow of conversation changes somewhat when, with a mand, *R* reintroduces her plan of getting married (9). *A*, responding to *R*'s repeated plan to get married, makes a series of plan (10, 11, 12, 13, 14, 15, 16) and transformation (17) statements specifying how *R*'s marriage should take place — these are, therefore, turnabouts. *R* agrees with *A*'s transformation in an acceptance statement that is a response (18), and the episode ends when *A* changes the topic in an unlinked utterance (19).

Method and Results

A total of twenty-four predominantly middle-class children enrolled in the University of Houston Human Development Laboratory participated in the study. Twelve four-and-a-half-year-olds and twelve three-year-olds were divided into same-age and same-sex dyads, the members of each dyad being friends with one another. There were, therefore, three boy and three girl pairs at each age level.

The children were observed and videotaped in a play room that was apart from the regular classroom but familiar to the children. Three corners of the room were arranged as kitchen, dress-up, and block corners, the fourth was used for the video equipment. The materials in the kitchen corner consisted of miniature replicas of a refrigerator, an oven, and a small table with two chairs. In addition, there were kitchen utensils such as pots and pans varying in size and quantity. The dress-up corner contained a wide variety of materials including clothes and bolts of fabric. The block corner had blocks of different sizes and shapes. The materials in each corner ranged from minimally to highly structured and were drawn from the everyday classroom. After they had become familiar with the investigators, the children were videotaped playing in this room in sessions of twenty minutes on each of two consecutive days.

The children's utterances and actions were transcribed as fully as possible to produce scripts for each dyad's two sessions. These scripts were detailed enough to permit each child's utterances and actions to be read in the full context of the evolving play interaction. Transcripts were prepared by the principal investigator and two assistants. In this process, following McLoyd (1980), the play was segmented into turns (defined as all of one partner's utterances before the other partner took the floor), these turns being comprised of utterances (defined as words or string of words or nonlexical items associated with a sound property of an imaginary or real object). A third assistant then reviewed four randomly chosen transcripts to establish reliability of turns and utterances and word accuracy. There was perfect agreement on segmentation of turns and 99 percent agreement on utterances and word accuracy. The principal investigator and a fourth assistant then independently classified all the utterances according to their conversational function using the four mutually exclusive categories described above. The mean percentage agreement on four randomly selected transcripts was 87 percent; the disagreements were then resolved by discussion.

The first general finding is that there was a good deal of speech in the play sessions, the older children being more verbal than the younger. The mean number of utterances for three- and four-and-a-half-year-olds were 372 and 603 respectively; that is, 9.38 utterances per minute for the younger dyads and 15.07 for the older. The mean number of turns taken by three- and four-and-a-half-year olds were 192 and 302 respectively.

In the first of several analyses based on relative frequencies we examined the distribution of all utterances in terms of their conversational function. The results of this $2 \times 2 \times 4$ (Age $\times$ Sex $\times$ Conversational Function) ANOVA, with four repeated measures on the last factor, are presented in Table 1.

The four separate tests of simple main effects on each conversa-

Table 1. Relative Frequency of Utterances in Terms of Their Conversational Function

	Conversational Function				Significant Findings
Age	Turnabout	Response	Mand	Unlinked Utterance	
3	.26	.35	.32	.07	Conversational Function: $F(3.24) = 40.09\ p\ (<.001)$
4½	.42	.29	.26	.03	Age × Conversational Function: $F(3.24) = 5.62\ P\ (<.005)$

sational function indicated that the older children made significantly more turnabouts and fewer unlinked utterances than the younger children. Further, we found that the four functional forms differed significantly from each other at each age level. T-tests made after the analysis of variance revealed that, at both age levels, turnabouts versus unlinked utterance, response versus unlinked utterance, and mand versus unlinked utterance comparisons were significant. Most interesting, while the older children made significantly more turnabouts than they did mands, this difference did not reach significance for the three-year-olds.

In a second set of analyses, we sought to examine what relationship might exist between the communicative and conversational aspects of the children's play dialogues. To this end we classified the statements in each metacommunicative category according to their conversational function; each plan, transformation, and so on was classified either as a turnabout, a response, a mand, or an unlinked utterance. In this contingent classification scheme, the analyses of plans, object statements, and transformations revealed the most consistent and the most interesting pattern. The results of these analyses are summarized in Table 2. Tests of simple main effects on each of four

Table 2. Relative Frequency of Plans, Transformations and Object Statements in Terms of Their Conversational Function

Age	Conversational Function				Significant Findings
	Turnabout	Response	Mand	Unlinked Utterance	
Plans					
3	.27	.11	.38	.24	Conversational function $F(3.24) = 13.29\ p < .001$
4½	.57	.02	.33	.08	Age × conversational function $F(3.24 = 4.97\ p < .008$
Transformations					
3	.24	.30	.40	.06	Conversational function $F(3.24) = 25.27\ p < .001$
4½	.50	.16	.32	.02	Age × conversational function $F(3.24) = 8.17\ p < .001$
Object Statement					
3	.25	.23	.43	.09	Conversational function $F(3.24) = 8.58\ p < .001$
4½	.54	.14	.30	.02	Age × conversational function $F(3.24) = 2.90\ p < .05$

conversational forms in these analyses indicated that the four-and-a-half-year-olds were more likely than three-year-olds to express plans, transformations, and object statements in the form of turnabouts and less likely to express them in the form of unlinked utterances. Further, looking within age groups, we found that the four-and-half-year-olds were more likely to express their plans as turnabouts but their object statements and transformations as turnabouts or mands. Three-year-olds, however, were equally likely to express their plans and object statements in any form. On the other hand, their transformations were more likely to be turnabouts, responses, or mands than unlinked utterances. (There were no significant differences between the first three functional forms.)

In summary, this second set of specific findings not only reinforces the general picture of the older children's play conversations being more coherent, but also adds some interesting detail to that picture. In particuluar, it seems there is a discernible and developing relationship between types of metacommunicative statements and conversational properties of preschoolers' play speech.

Discussion

We have sought to examine the question of how several different components of children's play context are connected in a dynamic fashion by identifying the conversational function of utterances in dyadic play. The main analysis of all preschoolers' utterances suggests the presence of a developmental trend toward greater conversational continuity and coherence. Interesting in itself, this finding might also be taken to have implications for the concept of social-cognitive development and for the way in which it can best be studied. We conclude with some speculations along these lines.

Kaye and Charney (1980) state that "the structure in which... expansion and clarification of the child's meanings takes place is the dialogue." In the present study we have attempted to examine the ways in which such meanings are expanded in play dialogues. That older children express their plans as turnabouts more than younger children suggests that these children explicitly connect their intentions about ongoing activities with their partner's previously expressed ideas. Similarly, the fact that object statements were more likely to be turnabouts for the four-and-a-half-year-olds indicates that in determining the possession of objects in play, the older children both refer to their partner's expectations and prepare a ground for the partner's restatement of his or her intentions or expression of new ones.

The findings on plans and object statements collectively present a picture of play dialogue in which, with increasing age, children explicitly establish relationships between each other's intentions in organizing the psychological and physical structure of play. Consistent with such results, the analysis of transformations suggests that there is a developing active interaction between the play partners, not only regarding their interpretation of play reality but also regarding how that is represented and expressed. It seems that children's knowledge and understanding of the social and physical world as expressed in transformations become constructed in an increasingly reciprocal way with increasing age.

As outlined in this chapter, the study takes an initial step toward describing the process by which children interact with and influence one another in the context of their imaginative play relationships. Based on these descriptive results, we cannot address the question of how different aspects of play context influence the degree to which children provide continuity in their play dialogues. It remains to be seen, for example, how play dialogues are shaped by varying degrees of children's familiarity with each other and with play materials, and how the nature of conversation interacts with play themes and with different phases in the evolution of a play relationship.

Clearly, if play dialogue is conceived of as a process by which participants actively orient themselves and others to meaning (Bruner, 1974/75; Sutton-Smith, 1980; Vygotsky, 1962), a complex array of interacting factors can be assumed to influence that process; the existing level of knowledge with which children come to the play environment, the features of the environment, and the goal of the activity will all have to be part of a full account of children's dialogues. More generally, such an account can best be seen as part of the contextual-event view of cognitive functioning expressed by Rogoff (1982):

> A contextual cognitive developmental theory would emphasize the following concepts: 1. Cognition is an activity or event integrating and depending on both the person and the context. 2. An examination of the processes of children's *adaptation to* (transformation in) their contexts is essential to cognitive theory. 3. Adaptation of person and context to each other implies that there is no unique or ideal end point to development. 4. Thinking is integrated with practical action. 5. Children play an active role in detecting information, exploring their environments, and creating solutions to problems in accord with the supports and constraints of the environment. 6. Cogni-

tive development depends upon children's adapting and adopting the intellectual tools and skills of the larger sociocultural context through social interaction guiding their activities with the material and social context [p. 154].

Finally, it seems to us that such a contextual-event view has direct implications for the study and analysis of both metacommunicative statements per se and their conversational function. Emphasizing the transforming character of social context, this view underlines the argument that metacommunicative statements (even a statement apparently repeated verbatim) will change in quality to reflect evolving intentions and expectations of children as the play interaction progresses. As a consequence, for the function of metacommunicative statements to be fully explicated they should be qualitatively analyzed as embedded in the total sequence of play interaction. It seems to us that the meaning of the integrated interaction can be kept intact and best explicated only through such qualitative analyses. Analyses based on quantified data, of the kind undertaken here, tend to divorce utterances from the total context in which they take place, thus tending to obscure the total conversational subtleties of meaning carried by the statements. In order to provide a faithful picture of the play partners and their evolving relationship we should examine the data in ethnographic, microgenetic terms (Rogoff, 1982; Kessel, 1980). Less than widely used in psychology, such an approach calls for qualitative narrative reporting of dialogues along the lines of our brief illustration and the form of interpretive, hermeneutic analysis well represented by Kelly-Byrne in Chapter Three of this sourcebook.

References

Bateson, G. "A Theory of Play and Fantasy." *Psychiatric Research Reports,* 1955, *2,* 39–51.
Brown, R. "The Maintenance of Conversation." In D. R. Olson (Ed.), *The Social Foundations of Language and Thought.* New York: Norton, 1980.
Bruner, J. S. "From Communication to Language: A Psychological Perspective." *Cognition,* 1974/75, *3* (3), 255–287.
Conrad, R. "The Chronology of the Development of Covert Speech in Children." *Developmental Psychology,* 1971, *5* (3), 398–405.
Dore, J. "Conversation and Preschool Language Development." In P. Fletcher and M. Garman (Eds.), *Language Acquisition.* New York: Cambridge University Press, 1979.
Elder, J., and Pederson, D. "Preschool Children's Use of Objects in Symbolic Play." *Child Development,* 1978, *49* (2), 500–504.
Ervin-Tripp, S., and Mitchell-Kernan, C. *Child Discourse.* New York: Academic Press, 1977.
Fein, G. G. "A Transformational Analysis of Pretending." *Developmental Psychology,* 1975, *11* (3), 291–296.

Fein, G. G. "Play and the Acquisition of Symbols." In L. Katz (Ed.), *Current Topics in Early Childhood Education.* Norwood, N.J.: Ablex, 1979.
Fein, G. G. "Pretend Play in Childhood: An Integrative Review." *Child Development,* 1981, *52* (3), 1095-1118.
Fein, G. G., Moorin, E. R., and Enslein, J. "Pretense and Peer Behavior: An Intersectoral Analysis." *Human Development,* 1982, *25* (6), 392-406.
Field, T., DeStefano, L., and Koewler, J. H., III. "Fantasy Play of Toddlers and Preschoolers." *Developmental Psychology,* 1982, *18* (4), 503-508.
Garvey, C. "Some Properties of Social Play." *Merrill-Palmer Quarterly,* 1974, *20* (3), 163-180.
Garvey, C., and Berndt, R. "Organization of Pretend Play." Paper presented at the annual meeting of the American Psychological Association, Chicago, 1977.
Göncü, A. "Development of Preschoolers' Imaginative Play: Cognitive and Communicative Aspects." Unpublished doctoral dissertation, University of Houston, 1983.
Göncü, A., and Kessel, F. S. "Transformational and Metacommunicative Analysis of Dyadic Play: A Developmental Study." Unpublished paper, University of Houston, 1983.
Jackowitz, E. R., and Watson, M. W. "Development of Object Transformations in Early Pretend Play." *Developmental Psychology,* 1980, *16* (6), 543-549.
Kaye, K., and Charney, R. "How Mothers Maintain 'Dialogue' with Two-Year-Olds." In D. R. Olson (Ed.), *The Social Foundations of Language and Thought.* New York: Norton, 1980.
Kessel, F. S. "Playful Precursors of Metacognition: An Exploration." Paper presented at the annual meeting of the American Educational Research Association, Boston, April 1980.
McLoyd, V. C. "Verbally Expressed Modes of Transformation in the Fantasy Play of Black Preschool Children." *Child Development,* 1980, *51* (4), 1133-1139.
Matthews, W. S. "Modes of Transformation in the Initiation of Fantasy Play." *Developmental Psychology,* 1977, *13* (3), 212-216.
Pederson, D. R., Rook-Green, A., and Elder, J. L. "The Role of Action in the Development of Pretend Play in Young Children." *Developmental Psychology,* 1981, *17* (6), 756-759.
Piaget, J. *Play, Dreams, and Imitation in Childhood.* New York: Norton, 1962.
Rogoff, B. "Integrating Context and Cognitive Development." In M. E. Lamb and A. L. Brown (Eds.), *Advances in Developmental Psychology,* Vol. 2. Hillsdale, N.J.: Erlbaum, 1982.
Rubin, K., Fein, G., and Vandenberg, B. "Play." In M. Hetherington (Ed.), *Handbook of Child Psychology,* Vol. 4: *Social Development.* New York: Wiley, 1983.
Schwartzman, H. B. *Transformations: The Anthropology of Children's Play.* New York: Plenum, 1978.
Sutton-Smith, B. "Children's Play: Some Sources of Play Theorizing." In K. H. Rubin (Ed.), *Children's Play.* New Directions for Child Development, no. 9. San Francisco: Jossey-Bass, 1980.
Sutton-Smith, B. "Piaget, Play and Cognition Revisited." In W. Overton (Ed.), *The Relationship Between Social and Cognitive Development.* Hillsdale, N.J.: Erlbaum, 1981.
Torrance, N., and Olson, D. R. "Oral Language Competence and the Acquisition of Literacy." Unpublished paper, Ontario Institute for Studies in Education, 1982.
Vygotsky, L. S. *Language and Thought.* Cambridge, Mass.: M.I.T. Press, 1962.
Vygotsky, L. S. *Mind in Society: The Development of Higher Mental Processes.* Cambridge, Mass.: Harvard University Press, 1978.

Artin Göncü is a research associate at the Center for Advancement of Child Care and Education and a lead teacher at the Human Development Laboratory, University of Houston. He received his Ph.D. from the University of Houston in 1983.

Frank Kessel is associate professor of psychology at the University of Houston. He received his Ph.D. from the University of Minnesota in 1969 and is coeditor of and contributor to The Child and Other Cultural Inventions.

Study of fantasy play as drama illuminates developmental differences in the elements of social knowledge and characterizes relations between these elements.

The Organization of Dramatic Content in Children's Fantasy Play

David Forbes
Gary Yablick

The distinction between *context* and *content* can be employed in various ways to characterize research on children's play. Many analysts of children's play stress that it takes place within an as-if context that insulates the players from real consequences of their actions. This use of the notion of context shapes the corresponding meaning of content in the analysis of play behavior. Specifically, research stressing the as-if context of play typically presumes that the content of play represents children's practice of activities similar to those they might engage in in the real world, as if those activities were real. Schwartzman (1976), for example, has examined how children use the as-if context of play to experiment with the social relationships they have with one another outside of play, and she suggests that children learn something about the nature of their social relationships as they engage in this experimentation. In their analysis of play behavior, Schwartzman (1976) and

---

This research has been supported by the people of the United States through grants to the first author from the National Institute of Mental Health and the National Science Foundation.

F. Kessel, A. Göncü (Eds.). *Analyzing Children's Play Dialogues.* New Directions for Child Development, no. 25. San Francisco: Jossey-Bass, September 1984.

others, making this context–content distinction, focus on the question, What is being practiced within the context of pretense?

Other researchers make a different distinction between context and content in their analyses of play. They view play as providing one type of context for real peer interaction. For these researchers, children are observed at play to determine how they orchestrate their interactive competencies to solve the interpersonal demands of one type of social situation — that of imagined play. For these analysts, the content of play is a corpus of real social interaction strategies. Using this perspective, Garvey (1974) has studied children's play as a context for learning about rules of conversation, including how children signal agreement, raise questions for clarification, and defend play ideas to their playmates. She has also examined communication concerned with signalling when action is to be considered pretending and when it is to be taken literally. For researchers who adopt this perspective of context and content, the basic research questions are, What types of social interactive challenges confront the child in the play context, and What strategies are adopted to meet these challenges?

World Building

In the work discussed in this chapter, we focus on play as a context in which children are "world building." We start with the general notion explicated by Goffman (1974) that social interaction always involves framing activity, by which the interactants develop a joint understanding of what is going on in their interaction. In the context of fantasy play, *framing* can take on a larger meaning than what it has in Goffman's treatment. As Goffman notes, framing activity in everyday social interaction is supported by numerous keyings which facilitate shared understanding because of the consensual implications these keyings have for many aspects of an interaction. In fantasy play, all aspects of the make-believe world are initially fluid. The identities of the actors, the nature of the scene, and the nature of the action can be invented by the players and need not be based upon any a priori consensual keyings that might otherwise constrain the nature of the interaction. Consequently, the task of framing in fantasy play literally becomes one of (1) constructing a scene, (2) populating it with characters, and (3) bringing it to life with action. The content of children's fantasy play, from the perspective of the play context, is a series of contributions which children make toward the construction of an imagined world. The question that we ask about play context from this perspective is, What is the general structure of children's fantasy worlds?

The Reality-Creation Paradigm. By virtue of this focus, our analysis shares some characteristics with what Franklin (1983) calls the "reality-creation paradigm," which emphasizes that "imaginative realities" created in play do not "merely reflect or communicate what is already known but are formulative, meaning creating" (p. 207). However, we also make certain inferences from children's fantasy play using assumptions that Franklin might treat as part of what she calls the "communicational paradigm," where play is viewed as a reflection of children's understanding of the real world. In particular, we hold that analysis of children's fantasy play can tell us something about their understanding of very general properties of the real world.

Within such a framework, our research employs a descriptive language that attempts to define the basic elements of structure in the content of fantasy play, and to characterize relations between these elements. Using this language, we investigate the structural parameters of fantasy worlds constructed by children of different ages, not merely to discover how they create their coherent imaginary realities, but also to learn about their understanding of real-world situations and the principles that make such situations coherent and interdependent. We agree with Franklin that the primary function of analysis of a fantasy about a restaurant is not merely to determine either the players' particular experiences with real restaurants or their understanding of specific social conventions and possibilities in such situations. In addition to revealing these findings, the general dramatic structure of a restaurant episode may yield information about the kinds of elements from which children's dramas are constructed and the relationships between these elements which create coherence in children's dramas. In short, as we view it, children's fantasy play is perhaps best described as a transformational activity. Children actively create the worlds of their fantasies, but they do not do so without basis. We assume that the general structure of these fantasy worlds is based on categories of social representation and principles of categorical coherence that reflect the particular child's understanding of the real world.

Our view of fantasy play also has implications for understanding its role in the child's development. We suggest that the transformational activities of children's fantasy play provide children with opportunities to learn something about how situations are organized, that is, about the nature of the principles that make either real worlds or imaginary worlds coherent. By transforming the real world in the creation of play themes and observing the consequences of these transformations in the organization of their imaginative realities, children can gain a sense of the implications that exist between different aspects of the world.

Viewed in this light, fantasy play can be considered a species of manipulative play, with learning through experimentation taking place by accommodation to the outcomes of one's experiments and by assimilation of new forms of organization into one's existing knowledge base.

One particular comment by Franklin (1983) seems worth noting since it suggests a rationale for the theoretical apparatus we employ in our analysis of children's fantasy play: "I do not find compelling evidence for the idea that, overall, there is a trend toward increasing 'realism' in pretend play. Rather, it seems to me that there is a trend toward greater *inner coherence* in both reality-oriented and fantastical play (as well as in mixed forms)" (p. 216).

Our data, discussed later, are consistent with this observation, but for now it will suffice to pose the question: If the trend toward increasing inner coherence of children's fantasy play is not simply a function of the increasing realism of their fantasy worlds, what principles do children employ to bind the elements of a fantasy into a coherent whole? Note that framing the question this way presumes that fantasy play themes can be analyzed into constitutive elements and requires identification of the principles of relation used to tie them together. In addition, our assumption that children's fantasy play reflects their understanding of the real social world and enables them to learn more about it implies that the principles of relation that provide inner coherence to their imaginary realities be similar, at least, to discoverable principles of the real world.

This representation of the problem raises an embarrassing question: If the primary goal is to learn something about children's experience and understanding of the real social world, and if, moreover, the principles that provide cohesion to real situations are assumed to be similar to those operating in fantasy play, why not simply examine children's real-world interactions to discover these principles, rather than take a less direct approach through the study of fantasy play? As indicated above, our answer is that children need to talk more explicitly about the nature of their imaginary worlds since these are not already shaped by any of the factors governing the course of real-world interactions, such as physical laws, the ordinary properties of objects, prescriptive social norms, typical social roles, and so on. The nonliteral character of objects, places, and actions used in fantasy play strips this interaction context of consensual keyings that promote shared understanding, and thus makes it necessary for children to stipulate not only the elements involved but also the principles they use to justify including or excluding elements and their characteristics.

Dramatism. The need for a descriptive language to characterize the general structure of drama in children's fantasies has led us to the work of Burke. His principle of dramatism (1968, 1969) is the most subtle and extensive approach exploring the nature of dramatic structure. His analysis employs a basic system of categories which he terms the *dramatistic pentad*. These categories — scene, agent, act, agency, and purpose — are themselves unremarkable; they are, as Burke (1969) and Kaplan (1983) have pointed out, the natural categories of our everyday, unreflective experience. They describe situations involving persons who act to secure particular ends by employing certain means. Two aspects of Burke's approach are, however, especially relevant to our concerns in this study.

First, Burke focuses on *ratio*, or relationships between the elements in a drama. The particular elements in a ratio are related by virtue of being appropriate to or fitting for one another. Thus, for example, "an 'agent-act ratio' would reflect the correspondence between a man's character and the character of his behavior (as, in a drama, the principles of formal consistency require that each member of the dramatis personae act in character)" (Burke, 1968, p. 446). This representation of what a ratio is should make clear why we are interested in the concept: Ratios are precisely the kind of principles of relation between elements of a drama that describe its inner coherence. By focusing on the relationships children stipulate between the elements of their fantasy dramas, we will learn about the principles which provide coherent structure to the world of their fantasy drama, and this should tell us something about their understanding of the real world.

The other aspect of Burke's approach of particular interest pertains to the legitimacy of our inferences from children's use of ratios in fantasy play about their experience and understanding of real-world social processes. We have proposed that what children create during fantasy play are literally dramas, all the elements of which can be characterized in terms of our descriptive categories (based on Burke's dramatistic pentad). Like Goffman (1974), Burke stresses the symbolic nature of all human interaction. In particular, he argues that a dramatistic analysis of this symbol system applies equally to the structure of formal dramas and to the nature of everyday interaction: "Man is defined literally as an animal characterized by his special aptitude for 'symbolic action,' which is itself a literal term. And from there on, drama is employed, not as a metaphor but as a fixed form that helps us discover what the implications of the terms 'act' and 'person' *really are*" (Burke, 1968, p. 448). This notion that children experience real social interaction in the same terms they use to create their fantasy dramas gains some measure of support from workers such as Garvey (1974) who note that explicit framing statements are often used to mark the beginnings and endings of fantasy play. If the symbol system of real-world interactions did not closely correspond to the symbol system of fantasy play, no such boundary markers would be necessary.

In summary, Burke's dramatistic perspective provides us with a system of descriptive categories for characterizing the dramatic content in children's fantasy play, and a way of analyzing such dramas in terms of their elements and the relations between them. This perspective also suggests a rationale for discerning social development as it is manifested in the structure of fantasy play dramas. We expected that an analysis of the types of elements to which children referred in shaping their fantasy play, and of the kinds of ratios which were recognized or posited between these elements, would yield descriptive information about children's understanding of regularities and relationships in social interaction.

Methods

Subjects for the study were five- and seven-year-old children from the Cambridge, Massachusetts, public school system. All subjects were normal in that they had never been identified as having psychological or educational difficulties. Children were transported to a laboratory playroom at the Harvard Graduate School of Education where they participated in after-school playgroup sessions. These playgroups consisted of six children per group, three girls and three boys. Each playgroup met for one hour per day for twelve days over a three-week period. Four groups are represented in the data presented here — two groups of five-year-old children and two groups of seven-year-olds.

Coding. The results reported here are based on a preliminary analysis of videotapes of the first and second play sessions, comprising eight of the total forty-eight playgroup hours. Each of the eight hours was transcribed by coders instructed to isolate interactions which referred to ideas for fantasy play and conversations which took place within the context of active fantasy.

The transcripts were coded on an utterance basis. For each utterance coders indicated which dramatic elements were explicitly referred to by the child and identified each element as belonging to one of five element categories. (The definitions of these categories and the principles for coder decision making are elaborated in a coding manual which is available from the first author.) A summary of the definitions for the five element categories appears in Figure 1.

Coders were also instructed to indicate when children made

Figure 1. Overview of the Dramaturgical Coding Scheme

Element Categories

1. *Character:* All references to person within a fantasy drama or traits and qualities of persons are assigned codes in the character category.
2. *Behavior:* All forms of action within the drama, overt or covert, are assigned codes within the behavior category.
3. *Scene:* All references to locations of action that are assigned names are coded in the scene category (that is, references to "over here" and "up on the top" are not coded as scenes).
4. *Purpose:* All references to goals of action or action sequences are assigned codes in the purpose category. Unstipulated use of purposive language (for example, "we need to go outside") would not be coded under purpose.
5. *Object:* All references to props that are part of the dramatic scene are coded in the object category.

Ratios

Ratios between element categories were coded whenever children made statements that referred to relationships of appropriateness or necessity that linked the categories. The following are examples of such statements and their coding.

1. *Scene-Behavior Ratio:* "This is a restaurant; you can't just stand around."
2. *Scene-Character Ratio:* "We can't have dinosaurs in the house."
3. *Character-Behavior Ratio:* "You can't beat up the Tyrranosaurus."

Ratios involving two elements of the same category were also coded, as in the following cases.

4. *Character-Character Ratio:* "The real Superman is stronger."
5. *Behavior-Behavior Ratio:* "We have to put on pajamas to go to bed."

---

statements that stipulated relationships or ratios between dramatic elements. These included cases in which elements were linked to one another by statements of necessity (for example, if scene is x, then agent must be y) or appropriateness (for example, action x is appropriate for agent y). Also included were cases in which children questioned another player's ideas for the fantasy by drawing attention to the inappropriateness of a dramatic relationship or its indefensibility on grounds of necessity.

We have found it useful to make a substantive modification of Burke's system of ratios. Burke (1969) considered only the "loose correspondences" between terms in different categories, sometimes using only the ten nonordered pairs (a scene-act ratio being considered the same as an act-scene ratio, and so on), and sometimes finding it useful to differentiate ratios by the order of their terms ("...by a 'scene-act ratio' one would refer to the effect that a scene has upon an act, and by an 'act-scene ratio' one would refer to the effect that an act has upon a scene" (p. 433); in this case twenty ratios can be enumerated. We have chosen to leave aside considerations of ordering at this stage of analysis, giving us only ten ratios between different types of elements. We have also decided to include the five ratios that pair elements of the same dramatistic category, i.e., scene-scene, behavior-behavior, character-character, object-object, and purpose-purpose ratios. Thus, for example, a child player's justification for excluding some character's behavior from a fantasy on the grounds that it is inappropriate in a drama containing some other behavior (either of the same character or of another) is treated as invoking a behavior-behavior ratio.

Coders were instructed to mark only those cases in which a child changed content in one of the element categories, either by introducing a new element (for example, a new scene or a new character) or by elaborating an old one (for example, saying new things about a previously introduced character). Definitions for each of the fifteen ratios which were coded for the analysis are available in the coding manual. This procedure yielded a total of 706 lines of coded fantasy conversation, with 1,027 separately coded element references, and 191 coded dramatic ratios or relationships.

Dramatic Cohesion. A second, less formal technique of data coding is also presented here. This technique was adopted to help us explore structure in children's fantasies at the level of the episode. To that end, we adapted the linguistic concept of *cohesion* (for example, Halliday and Hasan, 1976) which refers to the semantic connections between utterances of a conversation. Our analysis of dramatic cohesion sought to uncover how episodes of fantasy might be seen as having dramatic as well as semantic unity. The analysis explores the possibilities of characterizing entire dramas as "anchored" by one central dramatic element which provides the dramatic continuity of the episode. We selected relatively lengthy episodes of fantasy play for this exploration, to determine if they could be described as connected in terms of one particular focal element. This technique yielded examples of episodes anchored by a behavior element, episodes anchored by a scenic element, episodes anchored in terms of an overall purpose, and episodes anchored by a particular character. The results presented are based on a preliminary examination of twenty anchored episodes, half from the five-year-old subjects and half from the seven-year-olds. Figure 2 presents examples of each of these types of episode anchoring.

Results

The first analysis performed was a simple examination of the frequencies of the five types of dramatic element referred to explicitly by

Figure 2. Examples of Episode Anchoring

A. *Action Theme*
   1: I'm gonna stab you.
   2: No one can beat him up.
   1: He's gonna bite him.
   2: I gotta hide away.
   1: Hide, good guy!
   2: He cut off his head.
   1: I eat you up... he's dead.
   2: But these two dinosaurs are never gonna get dead.
   1: I'll bury this dinosaur but I won't bury this one.

B. *Scenic Theme*
   1: Pretend this was a restaurant. O.K.?
   1: I'll be the waiter.
   1: Excuse me, sit right...
   1: O.K., what would you like for lunch?
   1: This is a restaurant; you can't just stand around.
   2: Can I get it myself?
   2: I'll be the cash register.
   1: Why don't we both do it?
   2: What would you like?
   1: I want some coffee.
   2: How about pancakes?
   1: No, I guess some coffee.
   2: Eggs would be good for you.

C. *Character Development Theme*
   1: I'm the good Superman.
   2: I'm the bad Superman.
   1: I'm the real Superman.
   2: You want to know who the real Superman is, have a duel.
   2: Whoever can fly the highest, whoever is the strongest.
   1: The best Superman don't got loose stuff.
   1: So you're the fake one.

D. *Purpose Theme*
   1: Lookit, this is the family.
   2: She always comes over to play with them.
   1: They like coming over to each others' houses.
   2: Let me do your hair.
   1: We'd better hurry up and get ready.
   2: Get ready for what?
   1: So she can come over.
   2: Your cousin is going to come over.
   1: Let me do your hair.
   2: This time I keep still 'cause its my favorite hairstyle.
   2: Let me do your hair 'cause your cousin is coming over.

Note: 1 and 2 identify the play partners.

children in the course of their fantasy play. Table 1 presents these overall frequencies. As can be seen, there are two significant differences in the types of elements used most frequently as building blocks by our five- and seven-year-old dramatists. Five-year-olds seem relatively more concerned than seven-year-olds with the actions which take place within the fantasies. Seven-year-olds, by contrast, seem relatively more concerned with the purposes of fantasy actions. Overall, our group of five-year-olds made a greater proportion of references to scenes and objects, and a smaller proportion of references to character, than our seven-year-olds.

The second analysis focused on the types of relationships or ratios that children referred to in constructing their dramas. Table 2 presents the overall frequencies of different types of ratios that were employed by subjects in both of our age samples. This table also shows statistically significant differences between the two age groups. First, the seven-year-old children simply used a proportionately greater number of ratios in their fantasy play than the five-year-olds. Nevertheless, the five-year-olds were more likely than the seven-year-olds to mention ratios which involve how actions fit together, how actions are appropriate to the scenes in which they are performed, and how various types of agents or characters belong in various types of scenes. The seven-year-olds were more concerned with the appropriateness of the actions performed by different types of characters, and also with the consistency of the characteristics of various general types of character.

Our final analysis is essentially anecdotal but seems consistent

Table 1. Number of References to Individual Dramatic Elements: Age Differences

Element Type	Age Five	Age Seven	Significance[a]
Scene	73	28	.12
Character	134	168	n.s.
Behavior	244	150	.05
Purpose	8	18	.01
Object	120	84	n.s.
Total Elements	579	448	

[a] Tests for differences in the number of elements referred to in subjects' fantasy interactions were performed on individual proportion scores, considering each child's references to a given type of dramatic element as a proportion of his or her total number of references to dramatic elements. Mann-Whitney U tests were used in all cases except purpose, where the total number of elements made this procedure impossible. Results for references to purpose are based upon a chi-square analysis for group totals.

Table 2. Use of Dramatic Ratios: Age Differences

Ratio Type[a]	Age Five	Age Seven	Significance[b]
Behavior/Character	16	20	.07
Behavior/Scene	17	5	.05
Behavior/Behavior	21	6	.02
Scene/Character	7	0	.04
Character/Character	0	10	.001
Total ratios/total lines	109/449	82/257	.05

[a] Only the ratio counts which approached or reached significance are listed here. A total of fifteen analyses were performed reflecting all possible ratio types.

[b] All significance levels refer to the results of chi-square tests on total number of ratios observed in each age group.

with the portrait of children's dramatic efforts painted by the preceding results. Of ten anchored episodes examined in the fantasy play of the five-year-olds, all but one derived their cohesion by anchoring to an ongoing action or behavior in the fantasy or to a scene in which the action took place. Of the ten examples of seven-year-olds' anchored fantasy play, only half derived their cohesiveness from a focus on a behavior or scene; the remaining episodes were anchored by an elaboration of character or by the pursuit of a goal.

Discussion

At first blush the portrait which emerges from our findings appears not totally unfamiliar. Our younger subjects can be described as following a path of development that has been well documented in previous research, particularly in the area of person perception (see Peevers and Secord, 1973; Livesly and Bromley, 1973). This path involves moving from a preoccupation with the concrete and external aspects of the social world toward more abstract and psychological concerns.

However, a more careful consideration of our results suggests that they have more important implications about the nature of development in representation of the social world. The structure of fantasy play at age five revealed by our analysis indicates that persons and their characteristics—the historical organizing categories of social cognitive research—may not be the primary categories of social representation in early childhood. Rather, behaviors and scenes in which they take place appear to be the primary domains of dramatic symbolization in early childhood. These are the major focuses in five-year-olds' fantasy play, as well as the primary elements referred to when ratios are used to interrelate the elements of a drama.

If one regards fantasy play as reflecting what children know about the real world, our findings imply that it may be inappropriate to state, as researchers studying person perception have, that children characterize persons in terms of behaviors and external characteristics. Rather, children could more appropriately be regarded as using the categories of action and scene to represent their knowledge about human action; their representations do not focus on character at all. Our results suggest that children begin the construction of a symbol system for social interaction by learning general "scripts" of human action, (after Schank and Abelson, 1977) in which scenes and the actions appropriate to scenes are primary focuses while characters remain relatively one-dimensional. The focus on person categories in research on children's social reasoning may also have resulted in a premature conclusion about the level of concreteness characteristic of early childhood social cognition. While a representation of persons in terms of behaviors may be concrete, a system for representing the organization in terms of appropriate action sequences, and for representing the constraints on behavior enforced by the nature of the scenes in which they occur, can be as abstract as any trait notion for characterizing persons.

Our results on the structure of fantasy play at age seven indicate that person categories are just emerging as a central focus of representational organization at this age. Since we would maintain that the person category is not a central organizing term in early childhood, we are faced with the task of explaining its emergence in middle childhood. One suggestion essentially parallels past discussions of the emergence of trait concepts in the person perception literature. That is, children may adopt the category of persons as a central term—and also the category of motives, as our results suggest—because of the utility of person and motive constructs for organizing representations of human action. Children in middle childhood begin to appreciate the representational efficiency of using trait terms to refer to patterns of behavior by persons engaging in such behavior over time; they also learn that references to behavior may be made efficiently in terms of the motivational elements that can be imputed to persons as a function of their behavior sequences. It should be noted that our account is still different from that of the person-perception students. While they would characterize trait terms as a more abstract and efficient means for referring to persons, we would stress that references to persons and their characteristics may be a more abstract and efficient means for referring to patterns of behavior.

Our finding that seven-year-old children also made more references to ratios generally in the course of their fantasy play provides some confirmation of Franklin's (1983) view mentioned earlier. As she suggests, it would appear that our older subjects are indeed more concerned with the inner coherence of their fantasy; this concern takes the form of more frequent linkage between elements of a fantasy through references to ratios which tie the elements together.

Because of the equal emphasis we have placed on each of the five dimensions of human action outlined by Burke, our study of social symbolization in the context of fantasy play offers a broadened perspective on the nature of social-cognitive organization in childhood. To date, the heavy emphasis on the category of persons in this area of study has led to an unduly narrow research focus. Our results indicate that the person category may not play as central a role in the organization of early childhood social knowledge as past workers have assumed. Clearly, it is time for researchers to broaden the scope of their efforts at understanding the nature of social representation and its development. Studies of children's social understanding must account for the acquisition of knowledge not only about people themselves, but also about the complex interrelationships between objects, scenes, persons, behaviors, and motives which make up the world of human action.

References

Burke, K. *A Grammar of Motives*. Berkeley: University of California Press, 1969 [1945].
Burke, K. "Dramatism." Under entry: "Interaction." In *International Encyclopedia of the Social Sciences*. New York: Macmillan and The Free Press, 1968.
Franklin, M. "Play as the Creation of Imaginary Situations: The Role of Language." In S. Wapner and B. Kaplan (Eds.), *Toward a Holistic Developmental Psychology*. Hillsdale, N.J.: Erlbaum, 1983.
Garvey, C. "Some Properties of Social Play." *Merrill-Palmer Quarterly*, 1974, *20* (3), 163–180.
Goffman, E. *Frame Analysis*. Cambridge, Mass.: Harvard University Press, 1974.
Halliday, M. A. K., and Hasan, R. *Cohesion in English*. London: Longman, 1976.
Kaplan, B. "Genetic-Dramatism: Old Wine in New Bottles." In S. Wapner and B. Kaplan (Eds.), *Toward a Holistic Developmental Psychology*. Hillsdale, N.J.: Erlbaum, 1983.
Livesly, W. O., and Bromley, D. B. *Person Perception in Childhood and Adolescence*. London: Wiley, 1973.
Peevers, H., and Secord, P. F. "Developmental Changes in Attribution of Descriptive Concepts to Persons." *Journal of Personality and Social Psychology*, 1973, *27* (1), 120–128.
Schank, R., and Abelson, R. *Scripts, Plans, Goals, and Understanding*. Hillsdale, N.J.: Erlbaum, 1977.
Schwartzman, H. B. "Children's Play: A Sideways Glance at Make-Believe." In D. F. Lancy and B. A. Tindall (Eds.), *The Anthropological Study of Play: Problems and Prospects*. New York: Leisure Press, 1976.

David Forbes is an associate in the Graduate School of Education and director of the Peer Interaction Project at Harvard University. He received his doctorate from Clark University in 1981.

Gary Yablick is a graduate student in psychology at Clark University.

The nature and meaning of a play relationship can best be understood within its dynamic, historical context.

Text and Context: Fabling in a Relationship

Diana Kelly-Byrne

Context is not a difficult notion. It is one that we evoke in a quest for the meaning of texts, those about human behavior in particular. As texts stand in isolation, they are incomplete entities. Context is what molds, frames, and brings them to life. Like the notion of frame, context is an interpretive procedure which helps us to read the meaning of behavior — of human texts. Thus, a context is metacommunicative. It consists of premises, evaluations, associations, biographical factors, ecological factors, other facts from immediate surroundings, and intentions and rules about the behavior in which the participant in involved. However, as Bateson (1972) explained to his daughter who asked him about games, about being serious, and about the rules for games, the rules by which we interact with others in our constructions of reality are rarely like those which govern a game of canasta or chess. Rather, the rules change and are often undiscoverable, although we are constantly engaged in attempting to discover them.

From a phenomenological standpoint, participants create reality through their own constructions. As such, all meaning is seen as intersubjective and emergent in interaction. Thus, signals about meaning and about factors that shape the text are not only given, but dynamic and emergent in interaction. In such a theory of meaning, context is a processual and multiply layered notion. Furthermore, although always present, it is not always visible or audible. It is such a view of context that I hope to elucidate by describing the opening sequences of the first three encounters of a play/story event between a seven-year-old girl and an adult female investigator (the author). But before doing so, I wish to return to my opening suggestion that context is not a difficult notion, although it suffers from loose colloquial usage which tricks us into employing "context" to mean no more than situations.

Situation is usually taken to mean a cluster of given social information of an extralinguistic or extragrammatical nature which is also regarded as constant. Context, thus limited, is treated as a label for factors such as setting, topic, occasion, and social characteristics of participants such as sex, age, ethnic identity, education, and social class. The assumption made by those who take context to mean such situational factors is that once these factors surrounding the text are specified and known, they can then be used to elucidate any set of linguistic messages. Thus, context is treated as standing outside the linguistic or semantic process of communication.

However, when we see context as static, as not part of the ever-shifting linguistic process of reasoning, as being in the eye of the beholder rather than in the minds of the actors, we confuse the issue (Glassie, 1982). What is at once a simple yet powerful idea evaporates—in so studying context we enlarge and complicate the text we describe but probably come little closer to understanding it than when texts were studied in isolation. In contrast to this static view, I shall attempt to show how context is part of the total message from within an ongoing interactive situation, and how it is created and is part of the meaning of the event.

As shown in the case at hand, context is relative to the changing state of the relationship between the interactants. Changes in the relationship alter or modify the meaning of many of the initial contextual features that frame the relationship. I hope to show how difficult it would be to find any one set of extralinguistic factors that would sufficiently account for the subtle shifts in speech function and mood that occur within the encounters and that contribute to their meaning. Furthermore, it will be apparent how awkward it would be to explain fully some important early utterances made by the child participant in the present case without access to other "invisible" information that illuminates their meaning and even alters earlier interpretations. In fact, earlier texts themselves become contexts for later utterances, thus creating an interweaving of text and context. Such a dynamic view of context leads to the eruption of meaning not only within texts but between them as well. This is true of the three texts to be considered here.

The Study

Despite Bateson's (1972) clear indication that the metasocial character of play lies in the meaning given by participants to their constructions of reality, most of the focus in subsequent research has been on more obviously behavioral access strategies such as signals and faces, and on negotiations of physical phenomena such as the physical context and boundaries of the game. These constitute only limited aspects of what is intended by Bateson's notion of play as a kind of paradoxical framing. The typical behavioral technique of categorizing observed entry or boundary behavior, while illuminating in its own right, yields limited information about the meaning of the events to the participants.

In an attempt to enter more centrally into the subjective interpretations of context and text relationships, I participated in a play relationship with a seven-year-old girl (Kelly-Byrne, 1982). There were fourteen sessions of play with the child in her home, each lasting three to five hours approximately once a month for a year. The recording procedures were those used in ethnographic study (see Spradley, 1980).

The study is unique in that the investigator actively played with a child in the child's own territory for lengthy periods of time. The closest examples of such lengthy involvement come from the field of psychoanalysis or psychotherapy, although in such cases the child is taken to the therapist, plays in a strange space and does so within externally imposed time constraints, usually of about an hour. In the present study, by contrast, the child used a great variety of behaviors and showed much sophistication for framing her own play relationship. For example, she used rituals (Turner, 1974), game strategies (Goffman, 1967), narratives (Geertz, 1980), and dramatic play and festival play (Sutton-Smith and Kelly-Byrne, 1984). Each of these genres was itself a context for the particular events that diversely managed her relationship to the playing investigator and indirectly commented on relationships of her parents.

I shall now describe how the child, Helen, set about making a relationship with me, Diana, an adult. In particular I shall focus on how, early in the relationship, the child negotiated a context for fabling and for using a language of importance to her. By fabling I mean fantasy making and activity having to do with story, myth, adventure, science fiction, tales, and so forth. I shall show how her early negotiations were crucial to the meaning of the play event. I shall argue that play and other ludic activity, including fabling, were means to her most inner concerns as well as a mask for them. As such, her fabling functioned as a stepping-stone and passageway to what she most desired: a close and lasting relationship with the adult. This desire and goal were initially revealed during the first encounter, although not fully until later in the relationship. I will now turn to the beginning phases of the first session in the relationship to demonstrate how she negotiated a particular order of relationship, one where not only had fabling become crucial currency but where the texture created by the play of text and context was polyphonic.

Session One. It was 5 o'clock one summer evening when Diana first met Helen. As the child opened the front door and met the adult the following conversation ensued.

Text I, Part I

D: Hi! I'm Diana.
H: Um! Another Wonder Woman.
D: And you're Helen, right?
H: Um. Have you read the Bible?
D: Yeah, a lot of it.
H: I've read all of it (referring to the Old Testament which she held in her hand). Here, I'll read you some.

The child then duly turned to a passage from Psalms that she read somewhat stiltedly. She read the passage accurately, although with not much sense to it. She arbitrarily stopped at a certain point and looked at the adult. The adult complimented her efforts and asked whether she knew many of the stories in the Bible as well. The child said that she did, and laid the Bible on the settee, after which the following conversation took place.

H: What shall we do?
D: Would you like *me* to read you a story now?
H: No, I can read them myself.
D: Well, what would you prefer to do instead?
H: Don't you think we'd better get to know each other first?
D: Yeah. That seems like a good idea.
H: Okay. But then you have to come to my room.

The adult agrees to move to the bedroom. As the two participants walked up the stairs and stood on the threshold to Helen's bedroom, she stopped short. Turning to the adult, the child announced an interdiction:

> H: I tell no one my dreams, secrets, secret languages, or about my superheroes, so don't ask me about them.
> D: Okay. That's fine by me.... So what'll we do?
> H: We'll find something.

This was said as the participants entered the room. Once they were in the room, the child took off her shoes and after a brief pause, turned to the adult and said:

> H: Can you fly? See, you do it like this. (She twirled across the room as if flying. The adult, accepting the challenge, said:)
> D: I think I can.
> H: Do it.

At this, the adult followed the child in a flying movememt, while the child showed signs of enjoying herself. Helen continued flying to the accompaniment of whizzing noises and then once more interrogated the adult:

> H: Know who I am?
> D: No.
> H: I'm Beauty the Butterfly. (Pause) Now, I'm Golden Bird, Raven Helper.
> D: Boy! They're all pretty good at flying.
> H: Of course they are. They're superheroes.

This is followed by more flying activity.

> H: Anyway, have you been to B_____ (a jumble of nonsense).
> D: Where?
> H: To Balalulaland. (Sounded like that.)
> D: (Adult shook her head.)
> H: It's a country. (Pause) In this place they speak a secret language, many secret languages like... (At this point, the child uttered a further stream of nonsense syllables, interpolating the sounds of p and b at the beginning of words.) Do you know them?
> D: No. I don't know that land or that language. But I know some other secret languages.
> H: Which ones?
> D: Well, here's one called 'Pee' language.

The child giggled. The adult then shared a play language that she had used as a child. Helen laughed and wished to be taught the language. After the child had learned it, the participants used it to speak with each other for a while. For example, the adult asked her whether she was hungry and would like to have dinner. To this, Helen replied:

> H: No po. Up-eye we-pill te-pell you-poo when-pen Up-eye ap-am hup-un-gry-py.

Discussion

There were several stages in Helen's behavior. At the beginning there was a display which may be described as an access ritual. Acknowledgment was made of the other by each participant, although the adult's behavior was fairly conventional, whereas the child's was not. At this stage all of the responses but for the child's first statement were of a public nature. They were oriented toward competence: for example, the child's Bible-reading self, and the adult's move to read to her dictated by her own script about babysitting or child-adult interactions, which are befitting of preliminary interactions in a living room between a child and adult who have just met. However, Helen's negation of Diana's offer to read to her arrested this indirection of events. Instead of engaging in the kind of relationship that might have ensued had she accepted the adult's offer to read to her, Helen invited the adult to participate in a very different order of relationship. Helen's communication to Diana was an instruction about how she thought they should proceed in their relationship. This communication was further marked by a scenic technique when Helen suggested that Diana should go upstairs to her bedroom. In fact, this was a condition of proceeding with the order of relationship that the child wished to initiate. Here was the beginning of the child's negotiation of a relationship in which her definition of the situation obtained. Out of Helen's negotiation of a context, developments crucial to the meaning of this event emerged.

Having suggested that she would like to get to know the adult better and vice versa, and further, that this would only be possible in her own space, Helen then proceeded to instruct Diana about how to behave in her world. She did this by first talking about the nature of the world she wished to share with the adult. Second, she instructed Diana about the rules for acting within this world. This information was communicated by means of an interdiction. When Helen said: "I tell no one about my dreams, secrets, secret languages, or about my superheroes, so don't ask me about them," she signaled through this negation the assertion of its very opposite. She implied that what she and her adult partner could share in her bedroom was a ludic relationship rather than one which dealt directly with her fantasies, dreams, secrets, wishes, desired selves, and so forth, so the child insisted on an imaginary world. This was a metacommunication about the world she would create, the currency she hoped to use, and about her relationship both to the adult and to her own personal concerns.

Helen carefully introduced the world she wished the adult and herself to inhabit. However, she had no sense of whether Diana was capable of meeting the challenge. All she knew at the time was that her sitter was amiable and interested in her suggestions. Therefore, in keeping with her purposes, Helen proceeded to test and further instruct Diana on how to behave in relation to this world. For example, consider what the child did to delineate the context and nature of the relationship she wished to share with Diana. When Helen asked Diana whether she could fly she was, in effect, testing her. It was a trial to discover whether Diana could fable and engage in ludic activity. Helen needed to know this to learn whether Diana could be a participant in her world of fabling and fantasy. Notice the information Helen revealed about her world through her activity: She demonstrated flying; introduced Diana to the inhabitants who peopled this domain, such as Beauty the Butterfly, Golden Bird, Raven Helper, and such superheroes; and further, she implied that flying was a key characteristic of being "Super." All this information, which was to context their relationship, did not stand outside the lingistic and semantic process of communication between the interactants but was part of the communication.

Helen's first tests revealed that Diana could play. After all, she did fly. However, she tested her further, and this time, Helen wished to establish whether Diana knew about faraway lands and secret languages. With this inquiry the child was implying not only that actions and personages could be transformed in play but that places and communication systems could be too. In addition, the test suggests that Helen was preoccuped with secrets and Diana's knowledge about secret activity. Why might Helen be concerned with secrets, secret lands, and secret languages? It seems that in making a relationship with the adult, Helen was planning to share her more private self and its secrets with her. This is in contrast to the more public, Bible-reading self of the early stages of the encounter. To share this part of herself might after all be a precarious matter, especially given her partner's nonchild status, unless she could enter into collusion with her. Therefore, in order that they get to know each other better, it was important for Helen to discover whether Diana, in addition to being a competent play partner, could also be a worthy one, one who could be entrusted with secrets; with those dreams, fantasies and private revelations about the self. Such a contention about secrecy is borne out by later developments in the first session as well as throughout the relationship, and becomes a crucial part of the context for the child. Secrecy is part of their pact and also makes for exclusivity of the relationship. In the present session, only after Helen had made sure that the relationship as she wished it to be was viable — after Diana had passed the tests and initiation rites she had set her — did the child have good reason to believe that she had worked successfully to negotiate a context for play and its revelations. Significantly, it was after this that Helen narrated a story to Diana which was a fantasy autobiography. This was a disclosure of a more private self.

Text I, Part II

Helen began by mentioning a secret land. She emphasized to the adult that she knew this land, "the secret place, very well." This resulted in the adult enquiring how this was the case. The child's answer to this question is rather elaborate; it takes the form of a short narrative account:

> H: I know this land, Balalulaland, where they speak secret languages, very well. I was there as a baby. I grew into a very powerful princess with magical powers. I was invulnerable, the most beautiful girl. I could conquer everything. My father the king was dead. Killed by enemies... the Swabs. It was always war there and we had to make it peace. Be nice to everyone, care about people, like I did. Not like Michael who doesn't.
> D: Who's Michael?
> H: He's a boy in my school whom I hate. He's a tease. He doesn't like me.
> D: Doesn't he?
> H: No. I like teenagers like you. (Said quietly.)

This was a tale about magic, princesses, enemies, dead fathers, war, and revenge in far-off lands. She followed this by an allusion to the everyday world, in contrast to the fantasied Balalulaland, which enabled her to return to the everyday world as well as to make a revelation of a personal kind about her feelings for the adult. The story was about the self and her relationship to the adult which had been contexted by the earlier tests, rites, and instructions. It marked a further stage in the relationship and was contingent on the participants' prior behavior.

This story and statement of liking was then followed by an extended piece of make-believe play around a plot of good guys and bad guys that lasted about half an hour and involved animal superheroes. The make-believe drama ended by erupting into a spate of festival play in which Helen sang, danced, twirled about, lassoed imaginary horses, lifted her skirt as she circled around, and, in general, frolicked about. It seemed a fitting finale to an evening she had so carefully orchestrated. Both van Gennep (1960) and Turner (1974) make the point that ritual is transformative while ceremony is confirmatory. Having transformed her everyday relationship with the new babysitter from one of asymmetricality to one where they were partners in play, Helen was able to celebrate and thereby confirm her accomplishment in acts of playfulness which were contexted by all that had gone before.

Session Two. Session Two built on the first. Here too the agenda was making a relationship, although now the task was somewhat different from that of the first encounter: Since a particular order of relationship had already been initiated, the task at hand on this occasion was to re-establish and expand the relationship. The following is a transcript of the conversation that took place between Helen and Diana at the onset of this meeting.

Text II

Having rung the doorbell, I was met at the door and invited inside by Helen's mother who was accompanied by Helen. Helen said nothing when she saw me, but smiled shyly as she thrust a stick at me on which lay a green caterpillar, while her mother greeted me and told me of her plans. After the mother left the child began talking.

H: My new pet. Just found today.
D: Um. It's sweet. Let me have a closer look.
H: Where can I keep him?
D: What about any empty shoe box?
H: Um.... Come up to my room. (We go upstairs and I follow Helen to a corner of the room.)
H: See, here's what I have for it.
D: Oh! You do have a place for it. (The child had a box with leaves in it and a cover with some holes bored through the top.)
H: Yeah. (Laughs.) I think I'll let him sleep.
D: Okay.... Anyway, what have you been up to since I was last here?

H: Waiting for you. I've missed you. Where have you been?
D: I've had lots of work to do.
H: What work?
D: Oh, just work for the university.
H: (Pause.) Have you babysat anyone else?
D: No. Only my nieces.
H: Tell me about them.
D: What d'you want to know?
H: Well I mean, how old are they and what are their names? (Then with a mild laugh she added:) For a start.
D: Well, they're two and six and the younger one is Miranda and the older one, Selena.
H: What do you do with them? What do you play with them?
D: Oh, different games.
H Do you play superheroes with them?
D: No, I don't.
H: You mean you only play those games with me? Right?
D: Oh sure.
H: Okay. Er, what d'you want to do? (Paces about floor.)
D: I don't much mind. What would you like to do?
H: Well,... let's play that game. (Throws animals on floor.)

Only three sequences of behavior preceded the story enactment and fantasy making in this session. This minimum of negotiation at the beginning of the encounter is in contrast to the much lengthier preparatory episodes (about eight) which took place prior to the extended fabling that occurred on the first occasion. For example, the first episode was initiated by the child and carefully focused and bounded by the activity around the caterpillar. On this occasion Helen made a first contact with the adult by a smile and the gesture of calling attention to the green creature. The gesture of thrusting the stick at Diana served to achieve her purpose as she competed with her mother for Diana's attention early in the encounter. After her mother left, the child began to structure her relationship with Diana. She used her newly found pet to introduce a discourse topic for the purpose of re-establishing contact, for securing the adult's attention, and, more importantly, for inviting her up to her room. As Kenneth Burke (1941, 1966) would suggest, this was a rhetorical gesture in keeping with her intention to lure the adult into her play world where her private self stalked large.

The child's next move also worked toward creating a context for fabling. As we saw in session one, for Helen, fabling had its own physically marked space, and in keeping with this, on this second occasion too, Helen wished to move the adult from the foyer (a public space) to her bedroom (a private space and one associated with her fantasy world). To use Burke's terminology again, we might suggest that she accomplished this by using a question on scene (about where we could protect the caterpillar) to lead the adult to her room where an order of behavior different from that of the everyday would transpire. Further, this question was rhetorical as well in that Helen already had an answer to her problem. However, it was not real information that she sought but a means of engaging the adult's interest and for executing her fabling. The first sequence of activity was closed by Helen's decision to let the creature sleep.

The second episode of behavior was initiated by the adult. Now it was her turn to check out her relationship with the child as well as to take a turn at initiating a topic for conversation. Her somewhat broad question about what Helen had been doing resulted in a very specific and personal response. Helen directly acknowledged her warm feelings for the adult when she said she had missed her. This too is different from the child's initial response to Diana in session one, when she rejected Diana's first offer to read to her and proceeded to set up a series of tests for her. During that session personal sharing did not occur until some lengthy and elaborate preliminaries to play had been accomplished. On this second occasion, however, there was no need for such preliminaries; the first session had already accomplished that task. So in this encounter, even prior to the play there was an exchange of statements of a personal order. It was not the adult's competence that was now at issue but rather her feelings for the child. Accordingly, Helen's rhetoric sprang from the personal sphere as she sought to persuade the adult that she needed her, which is in contrast to the rhetoric of initiation and testing used on the first occasion. For example, here the child enquired about competitors for the adult's attention and emphasized her need to be special and central to her. She sought affirmation of their ludic sharing as exclusive. Such negotiations validate the claim that the shared and close relationship was being sought and established by the participants during the first encounter. To return to the text, this second sequence of behavior ended with both participants having made their feelings explicit, thus reassuring each other of a shared affective frame of reference from which they could then proceed.

The third sequence, marking the last juncture in the occasion, dealt with Helen's attempt to shift their interactions from those of the everyday world to those of the play world. Although it was she who once again initiated this move into the play domain, on this occasion she did so by inviting the adult to suggest the type of activity in which they might engage. This was in contrast to her behavior on the last occasion, when the adult was predominantly a bystander to and follower of the range of expressive activities the child initiated without consulting her (flying, secret languages, and so on). However, given the adult's reluctance to initiate action and take a lead—which was part of her own agenda for the occasion—Helen suggested her own scheme of action. After some deliberation she suggested that they "play that game." Notice that already there was a reliable stock of knowledge at hand that the participants could assume (Schutz, 1976). The game was what they had played on the last occasion and took the form of an improvised fantasy enactment about good and bad animals and superhero animals. Once again, we see how the relationship, its renewal and renegotiation, was essential to the child as well as the adult and an integral part of the context for fabling. What this suggests is that for this child (as for others, I suspect), valued and serious pursuits, whether they be fabling or anything else, may proceed only after a particular order of relationship has been negotiated and certain preliminaries have been undertaken.

Session Three. The third meeting is contexted by the earlier sessions and was an occasion for more direct and risky expression of the child's concerns—in this case, her fantasy play. Thus it is striking that upon arrival at this meeting, the adult immediately oriented to Helen's play world. Consider the following transcribed text of the beginning exchanges.

Text III

I visited Helen for a third time three days later. On this occasion, I arrived at about 5:00 P.M. As I waited for the front door to open Helen crept up on me and flung a rope around me. Laughing, she led me out to the backyard rather than to the house as usual.

H: (Flings rope around Diana and leads her to backyard, laughing.)
D: (Startles. Joins in play act. Struggles and walks behind child resistently as if a prisoner.)
H: We're going to a secret place. (Said on way to backyard.)
D: (Looks scared and somewhat suspiciously at child but says nothing.)
H: (Laughs and then begins to talk about the television program "Wonder Woman." As we reach the backyard, the child lets go of the rope, places my bag in a corner, and leads me to the back step, where she sits down. She con-

tinues:) It's my favorite show. I never miss it. But I don't watch much television, not as much as my friends. (She then began talking about the details of the plot in the last episode of "Wonder Woman" but then stopped abruptly and said:) Let's play, okay?

D: Okay.

H: (Helen then set up a game influenced by the last episode of "Wonder Woman" when she cast the adult as Wonder Woman among other superheroes such as Batman. She said:) You'll be a good Wonder Woman 'cos you look like her... I mean in real life.

D: Do I? (Looks puzzled.)

H: Yeah. You know, like Linda, the one who lives in New York. I mean, not Diana in the show but the one who acts Wonder Woman.

D: Oh. (Nodded head indicating that I knew what she meant.)

H: Okay. Now I have all the power of every superhero living including Wonder Woman.

D: Okay.

H: You'll be in this room, it's underground, with this *bad* guy. He's an evil robber. And like robbers he'll find ways of breaking out and you will have to fight him right?

D: Uh huh.

H: I will always come to save you and victor [*sic*] the robber. Now let's go. (Throughout the latter part of the conversation Helen kept striking the air with twigs and sticks she's picked up from the yard. She seemed pleased with the sounds she generated. She then twirled the rope which she'd earlier thrown over the adult and with a final flourish said:) For capturing robbers.

As the above suggests, the adult was immediately oriented to Helen's play world. There were no preliminary negotiations from the everyday world on either participants' part. Instead, Helen's gesture of stealthily creeping up on Diana and imprisoning her was one that immediately assimilated her into the play domain. So in contrast to both prior occasions, here her access ritual was a play gesture which was duly reciprocated by the adult. This was now possible because the participants had become partners in play. In the light of this it seems that we must modify Schwartzman's (1978) claim that negotiations *always* precede play and reconsider the implication from Goffman's (1959) work that it is always necessary to manage situations first.

Although this is true of encounters with strangers, among friends topsy-turvy play gestures can provide the initial orientation to contact. I suspect, however, that this only becomes evident in long-term relationships which are intensively studied and described.

Conclusion

The three texts considered here demonstrate that children, as much as adults, act to achieve certain ends in an interaction and accordingly generate discourse that influences and shapes the meaning of the event. As part of this process they create and bring to the foreground the context for their behavior. In this case, Helen made it quite clear by her actions that the adult and she were to be play partners. Through her behavior she was creating a context for the various stages of the relationship. This was occurring moment by moment and was influenced not only by her purposes but also her sense of story and drama, of fantasy and play, and by her decision to turn this babysitter— who struck her initially as "another Wonder Woman,"—to her own interests. Thus, what mattered in this situation was not merely what surrounded Helen's performance in the world. What effectively surrounded the performance in her mind is what influenced the creation of the texts. That is what is referred to as context (Glassie, 1982).

One of the reasons we assume context to be an unshifting and distinct parameter—a given—seems to rest in our understanding of phenomena coming after the fact. Further, given the often academic and rarefied nature of our thought, we tend to lose the emergent characteristic of human behavior, which is far less firm than we pretend in our carefully structured representations. In a situation such as the present case—establishing a new relationship—the meanings that are being forged and contexted are, in a sense, open to interpretation. In the experience of the here and now, contexts congeal moment by moment.

Finally, although it might seem that this study can be dismissed as a highly subjective rendering of a single case, the findings are very much in accord with a number of recent large-scale studies. These studies show that when children are observed with their best friends, they are much more capable of higher-level imaginative behavior than when observed in more usual experimental settings (see Rubin and others, 1983). Furthermore, this is thoroughly in keeping with current revisions of Piagetian research that suggest that when studies are executed in natural contexts, children perform at a much higher level than they did in Piaget's experimental work (Gelman, 1978). The most direct empirical implication of the present study, however, is that we have hardly even begun to fathom children's competence at creating and managing context.

References

Bateson, G. *Steps to an Ecology of Mind.* New York: Ballantine, 1972.
Burke, K. *The Philosophy of Literary Form.* Berkeley: University of California Press, 1941.
Burke, K. *Language as Symbolic Action: Essays of Life, Literature and Method.* Berkeley: University of California Press, 1966.
Geertz, C. "Blurred Genres: The Refiguration of Social Thought." *The American Scholar,* 1980, *49* (2), 165–179.
Gelman, R. "Cognitive Development." In M. R. Rosenzweig and L. W. Porter (Eds.), *Annual Review of Psychology.* Palo Alto, California: Annual Reviews, 1978.
Glassie, H. *Passing the Time in Ballymenone.* Philadelphia: University of Pennsylvania Press, 1982.
Goffman, E. *The Presentation of Self in Everyday Life.* New York: Anchor Books, 1959.
Kelly-Byrne, D. "A Narrative of Play and Intimacy: A Seven-Year-Old's Play and Story Relationship with an Adult." Unpublished doctoral dissertation, University of Pennsylvania, 1982.
Rubin, K., Fein, G., and Vandenberg, B. "Children's Play." In E. M. Hetherington (Ed.), *Handbook of Child Psychology. Social Development.* Vol. 4: New York: Wiley, 1983.
Schutz, A. *On Phenomenology and Social Relations.* Chicago: University of Chicago Press, 1976.
Schwartzman, H. B. *Transformations: The Anthropology of Children's Play.* New York: Plenum Press, 1978.
Spradley, J. P. *Participant Observation.* New York: Holt, Rinehart and Winston, 1980.
Sutton-Smith, B., and Kelly-Byrne, D. *The Masks of Play.* West Point, N.Y.: Leisure Press, 1984.
Turner, V. *Dramas, Fields and Metaphors: Symbolic Action in Human Society.* Ithaca, New York: Cornell University Press, 1974.
van Gennep, A. *The Rites of Passage.* M. Zedom and G. Caffe (Trans.) Chicago: University of Chicago Press, 1960.

Diana Kelly-Byrne received her doctorate from the University of Pennsylvania in 1982. She is director of the Program in Children's Literature and Imagination at the Graduate School of Education, University of Pennsylvania, and recently coedited The Masks of Play.

We stand at the threshold of an intrusion into social science by modes once known as literary or esthetic or ludic.

Text and Context in Imaginative Play and the Social Sciences

Brian Sutton-Smith

The most useful approach to take in this chapter is to deal with each of the three pivotal terms, *text*, *context*, and *imaginative play* as perspectives on this volume and on each of the papers.

Of the three terms, text has the oldest history, beginning with religious texts, followed by Renaissance musical texts, and finally, legal texts. The notion that human interactions are also a kind of text is attributed to romanticism and in particular to Dilthey (Bernstein, 1978). His view that understanding and interpretation are central to human affairs is the focus of the modern phenomenological hermeneutic movement with which we associate the names of Husserl, Heidegger, and Gadamer in Europe and Schutz and a variety of ethomethodologists and ethnographers in the United States (Bernstein, 1978). What was once seen as written down for interpretation and understanding—a very theological, legal, and literary preoccupation—is now seen as something we do with human interaction and human cultures, which are also to be "read" like texts. The fact that the present volume has as a major focus *text* (and is making no reference to reading or the curriculum) is a sign that literary and hermeneutic philosophical modes of thought are penetrating the tough integument of psychology.

The word *context* also derives almost entirely from interpretive rather than natural science assumptions and is usually a foreign term in psychology, except when it deals with something external and physical. In the practice of interpretive science, on the other hand, context can mean the verbal context of the interactees, but it can also mean their extralinguistic happenings, their ritualized social happenings, or the way interactees frame the current situation psychologically in terms of their own characteristics, memories, competences, habits and, more importantly, their own metaphors. Furthermore, context is an active term. The numbers of a group are constantly contexting their own affairs, constantly communicating with each other and interpreting each other and themselves to provide the meanings of the occasion which allow them to proceed. The notion of context is thus a thoroughly sociocentric notion.

Catching *imaginative behavior* in these particular nets of text and context can hardly be easy, particularly becuase imaginative behavior is what Hall (1969) would have called an activity of low rather than high contexting. High-context activities bring their own settings, scenarios and audience expectations with them. Thus sports or symphony concerts or congressional debates are high in context and therefore in predictability. Imaginative play is a low-context activity, therefore hard to predict and responsive in a labile way to wayward stimuli. Anything can happen. The aim of this volume has been to explore what does happen. But first, so that the above remarks and those to come are made clearer, the contrast between natural and interpretive science needs further illumination.

The Natural Science Context

Natural science, interpretive science, and mixed contexts are all represented in this volume. The theory of natural science implied is, roughly speaking, the theory which holds that social science parallels the physical sciences and that its assumptions and procedures, therefore, can be somewhat similar to those of the physical sciences. With due apologies for the simplicity of these statements, this approach may be said to imply that humans live in a lawful universe and that human behavior is predictable at least in the probabilistic sense. The function of a science is, therefore, the quest for laws, demonstrated through the prediction of behavior, and discovered wherever possible through experiment; but when that is not possible, discovered through correlational techniques. It is assumed that because such a lawful universe exists beyond the laboratory one can metaphorically dip into it with one's measures, or represent it in one's experiments. The artificiality or abstracted nature of these samples will still yield valuable information because of the constancies in the phenomena being sampled, much as the blood in a sample will not be fundamentally different from the blood in the body from which it is drawn.

It follows that the human subjects of our studies will be seen in the natural view as objects for study, and the contexts in which they exist will be regarded as another class of objects for study. The concern in this volume is with the existence of stable interactions between classes of objects defined by age and by sex and by several categories of communicative phenomena. Unfortunately, the very nature of this kind of empirical, correlational research means that one either does or does not find relationships of varying strengths, but can never, at least in that particular study, know what the nature of the relationship actually is — because one has already selected the variables and predefined one's understanding prior to the study. Therefore, text and context relationships can be discovered but are not easily interpreted in this kind of research. Such studies would be enhanced if the investigators also did a sufficient amount of preliminary observational work to assist in their own interpretations of the correlations discovered and to feed their own subsequent studies.

The Interpretive Science Context

The fundamental assertion of interpretive science is that since meaning is the central issue in human affairs it should also be the central issue in the scientific study of humans. This approach is associated with a myriad of concepts differentially distributed amongst many different kinds of social scientists. One most often encounters the following standpoint commitments: (1) the approach must be based on the subject's view of what is meaningful as well as that of the scientists (emic, not etic, study); (2) what is studied is always fundamentally social or relational and not individual in character, as is usually assumed in psychology; (3) the social construction of reality is not only what the investigated persons are engaged in but also what the investigator is doing; and (4) construction of reality is always an ongoing, unpredictable diachronic or processual matter in which the investigators are themselves involved. Knowing what the investigator is contributing to the investigative outcomes is just as important as describing what is happening. Interpretive science thus becomes a reflexive science, in which the investigator is required to make as explicit as possible both the presuppositions involved in the study and the ongoing influence of the investigator in the activity itself.

Another exciting aspect of this approach to science is that one currently finds not only philosophers but also literary critics and social scientists debating the same issues of text and context. The basic argument in such circles is over how much of what occurs in a given event resides in the text (thought of perhaps as a set of material and dramatic structures), and how much of the event resides in the structures of the context. But what contrasts most obviously with the natural science approach to the same phenomenon is that here the context is thought of as something that issues forth from the performance itself. It is in the antecedents and the intentions of the performers, not in something external to them. The context is a meaning framed by those being studied; it is the meaning they impose upon their activity.

While different investigators adopt different positions on these issues, Bateson's explication (1972) seems the clearest in bridging the natural science and interpretive science models. He says: (1) that actors have psychological *frames* which influence their interpretation of context, and (2) that *contexts* also exist with a certain amount of autonomy which signal to actors which frames are appropriate for them to use. But he also argues that realities are multiple and that communication can and will occur simultaneously at several levels (including that of the investigators); further, that one must try to assess these multiple patterns of meaning through time.

A Commentary on the Chapters in this Sourcebook

These remarks will help to frame my brief comments on each of the chapters in this sourcebook and indicate more explicitly why I am sometimes critical and sometimes impressed.

Göncü and Kessel. Chapter One dealt with the contexts of conversation and communication of play themes. It did not deal with the themes themselves: Thus, it did not deal with imaginative play as text. The contextings discovered showed that as children grew older they communicated more explicitly and organized more coherently. I found most interesting the confirmation of Corsaro's (1979) work showing that most of the play access for younger children was unmarked by explicit verbal negotiation. In addition, Göncü and Kessel's largest category quantitatively was that of transformations, which accords with Bamberg's (1983) work showing that in the very young, the metaphorical activity of transformation itself carries the bulk of communicative intent. With these young children the imaginative theme of transformation was itself both text and context. This is a very important point because we have to be careful about false separations of text and context, that is, treating the messages about the play as if they are radically separate from the play itself, which they sometimes are but sometimes are not. Bateson, with all his proxemic and extralinguistic knowledge, never did imply that the message "This is play" needs to be verbal. In early childhood the implicit markers of play are often exaggeration, miniaturization, and iconic noises and faces which are both text and context, as one clown invites another to join the dance. In this paper, however, I am mostly impressed with the increasing category refinements that Göncü and Kessel have brought into focus through their analysis of prior work both in communication and dialogue.

Forbes and Yablick. In Chapter Two, we are told to pay attention not to the communicational contexts (of language and pretense) but rather to the intrinsic nature of content—the text itself. This kind of abstraction of context from text, or of text from context, is an empirical mistake. It is the wrong move to make if we wish to learn more about play.

I was excited, however, about the emergence of Kenneth Burke on the interpretive scene, having myself tried to use Burke's grammar similarly in a 1959 paper analyzing the character and variety of one of New Zealand's most popular children's games (Sutton-Smith, 1959). I made the same mistake as Forbes and Yablick—separating Burke's grammar in *The Grammar of Motives* (1969) from his work on rhetoric, *A Rhetoric of Motives* (1974). Burke's theory is sometimes known as a theory of *symbolic action*. Like Forbes and Yablick, I thought one could talk about the symbols without talking about the action. Of course one can do what one pleases, but doing that would not be consistent with Burke. (Still, it is not easy to understand Burke. I was in a literary audience when a Burke advocate was admonished for Burke's incoherence, to which he replied, "Burke is neither coherent nor incoherent—he is beyond coherence.")

One does not, apparently, read Burke lightly without considerable literary background. What Burke always wanted to know, I believe, was what difference it made that you used this or that category. Where did your symbols get you? You cannot possibly answer this question unless you put the imaginative content back into the communicational context and ask which children were leading which other children in what particular direction, as well as why they all enjoyed that direction anyway. Sometimes play is pure politics, sometimes it is pure symbolism. For the first you need some Bateson, and for the second you need some Freud or psychodynamic theory. But mostly some kind of mix of the two is needed, since Bateson makes too much of play's paradox, and Freud too much of its disguise. However, I can not see much progress in play studies for those who avoid either one or the other or both (Sutton-Smith and Kelly-Byrne, 1984a).

Nevertheless, what impresses me about the Forbes and Yablick chapter is the substitution of a coherence theory of truth for the usual correspondence theory. Thus, the authors give priority to the play representations rather than to the real world they are supposed to represent. I am also impressed by their way of conceptualizing the shift from behavior/scene representations to person representations. This analysis corresponds neatly with my own earlier analysis (Sutton-Smith, 1981) of the growth of central person games as the focal social event of this period of childhood. Let me congratulate these investigators, then, for having the considerable courage to borrow from literary theory in order to solve the psychologist's problem. The times are ripe for such remarriages of literary theory and psychology.

Kelly-Byrne. In Chapter Three the presuppositions are those of interpretive science; the contexting is carried on by the two participants as they struggle with each other for the meaning of the text, and the text itself is the ritual, initiations, secrets, testings, narratives, enactments, and festival behaviors that they pursue. This chapter makes clear that one can separate the earlier phases of contexting (ritual, initiation, and so on) as some kind of precursor from its outcome, the imaginative or dramatic play; and then one can separate that dramatic play from its outcome, the festival play. It is as if there is some built-in chronology of a relationship emerging in this account.

Further, to go beyond the data presented here by Kelly-Byrne in order to make clearer the larger significance of her work, it is worth noting that as the year progresses, the narrative becomes substituted for play; and at the end of the year conversation is substituted for narrative. The quite radical epistemological possibility that comes out of this finding is that imaginative play is an archaic language for the expression of enactive meanings which, when the play collaborators achieve the communality that they did in this relationship, can become a passageway to a more articulate conversational language within a new and intimate relationship. The ludic relationship gives way to the intimate relationship. Having assumed it to be some kind of ultimate ontology, I am still in culture shock from the empirical outcome of this singular study. Frankly, I do not like the conclusion—that play is only a passageway to something else which is more significant. My compromise at this point is therefore to suggest to myself that this kind of passage seldom occurs and that most of us are stuck for life with our archaic ways of playing.

But the methodological issues are also important here. Methodologically, an originally enactive contexting by the participants is converted to texts by notes and tape recorders, and is then reviewed by many others who recurrently reinterpret the text and the original contexting. What begins as a highly subjective engagement becomes in time an increasingly public and self-consistent document, though still quite variously interpreted by those who are of different literary, therapeutic, or anthropological backgrounds. Given the flux of human meaning, only partial coherence is possible between all those who view a given series of human events. What we need beyond that partial coherence is some study of the way in which perceived differences, nevertheless, sometimes seem to resonate sufficiently with each other to heighten our sense of the reality of the varying interpretations, rather than giving us a sense of incoherence and unreliability. It is not sufficient to say, as Gadamer (1982) does, that once the event is over it has become history and is subject to endless reinterpretations. We also need to know why we often seem to have more faith in some of these interpretations than in others.

It seems unfortunate that whereas most natural (social) scientists are in outstanding command of such verification processes but often do not have much cogency in their interpretations of the received results, the interpretive scientists, for their part, give cogent accounts but just as often seem insufficiently concerned with verification. One could, for example, cite the differences between articles in psychology journals and those in anthropology journals as illustrations of this difference. In the present case, Kelly-Byrne's text takes on a coherence and authenticity of its own that makes it an important contribution to the literature.

Research on Play in this Century

I will now context historically some of the ways in which I see these two different empirical approaches, natural and interpretive, dealing with the subject matter of research on play throughout this century.

Natural Science. I begin with natural science and will seek to make the case that, in its study of play, natural science has been a thoroughly culturally relative science. It has focused only on those kinds of play which would support certain cultural presuppositions and has ignored almost entirely those that would not support those presuppositions.

My thoughts here are very much affected by the recent analysis of Spariosu (1982), who suggests that from the time of Platonic thought we have been dominated by a view of the world which has made play, literature, and esthetics secondary to science, logic, and philosophy. In this rational view of the universe, the best that these secondary subject matters could hope for would be to function as imitations of the more rational order of things, provided by science, logic, and philosophy. The best thing that play could do would be to imitate the more rational aspects of human behavior. It can be argued that the natural science play theories of the past one hundred years have clearly accomplished this rational Platonic wish. Such theories begin with Spencer, who connects play with evolution, and continue with Groos, who defines play as a form of preparation for adult life; Freud, who uses it to master anxiety; Erikson, who sees it as a counterpart to adult planning; Piaget, who makes play the place to consolidate more rational accommodative activities; Berlyne, who allows that in exploration and play one discovers the stimulus world; Bruner, who finds that problems are solved there; Liberman, who finds that the playful ones are the creative ones; Singer, who declares that those with imagination are better than those without it; and Bateson, who suggests that play is the original kind of metacommunication, without which ordinary communication is simply impossible and the social construction of reality hardly conceivable (Sutton-Smith and Kelly-Byrne, 1984b). From all this a skeptic might see the history of the scholarship of play in the present century as a steady idealization of hitherto unacceptable subject matter.

One way in which natural science scholarship has accomplished the sanitization of the phenomenon is by studying play in highly supervised situations such as nursery schools, laboratories, and clinical and supervised playgrounds. Children in nursery schools have constituted the largest source of play studies. Naturally, the aim of the majority of nursery school teachers must be to rule out of court the irrational and immature aspects of behavior, and they must go to great lengths to see that what occurs there is only "good" or "clean" play. It is their duty to socialize and to counter examples of irrational play. While I do not quarrel with this, I must argue that one gets a very limited view of what children's play is about from such contexts.

Not surprisingly, given the socialization orientation of most researchers in child psychology, most studies of preschool play have been studies of the way in which some measurement of play correlates with other measures of maturity or cognitive activity. The early childhood play literature thus pays extraordinary attention to such hypotheses of socialization as: (1) The kind of social organization of the players (solitary, parallel, associative, or cooperative) is linked to some other index of maturity (usually age, but sometimes intelligence or socioeconomic status); (2) better attached children play in more mature ways; (3) children of divorced parents play in less mature ways; (4) young girls play with more imaginative maturity than boys; (5) the structure of toys can affect the maturity of the play; (6) children who play together continuously with peers of the same sex play in more mature ways; (7) linguistic maturity and symbolic play maturity are correlated; (8) playful children are more creative; (9) imaginative children are less aggressive; (10) lower class children are, or are not, less imaginative (a matter of dispute); and (11) children in their home setting play at higher levels of maturity than the same children playing in public settings.

Viewing play thus — largely in terms of its correlation with other measures of maturity — is clearly consistent with the view that it has some rational (functional) role to play in this world. Unfortunately, there is a great deal of other information about play, not the kind studied in psychology, which suggests that a great deal of it is quite irrational and even dysfunctional. Children's folklore, for example, can provide us with a great deal of at least anecdotal documentation of the nature of play during childhood (for example, the early work of Opie and Opie (1968), and more recently of Sluckin (1982) in his study of Oxford playgrounds). My *History of Children's Play* (Sutton-Smith, 1981) and the accounts of Knapp and Knapp (1976), of Jones and Hawes (1972), of McDowell (1979), and others in the United States all make it clear that children's collective play is a world of power politics, of incredible struggle, of aggression, of sexuality, of parody, of regression, and many other nonidyllic matters.

The major meaning of social play that emerges from a review of folkloric material is that play is about power and the struggle for identity within the dominance-subordination domains of one's peers. This is simply not the same kind of play that prevails in supervised preschool play contexts out of which have come most descriptions of play in child psychological research — nonliteral, flexible, positively affected, and intrinsically motivated, to cite a recent example (Krasnor and Pepler, 1980). In a context in which one is largely guarded from the worst excesses of other children, these attributes might well be useful in describing play. But in unsupervised peer play none of them need be of importance, although of course they can be. Often, in street play, the extrinsic motivation to belong to the group leads to play that is not freely chosen; in such play there may be victimization, scapegoating, and unkindness. The affect can be quite negative. In addition, the behavior is sometimes extremely routinized. In such a world of peer power politics — even when games are involved—it is very difficult to see nonliterality as a simple concept.

For example, Hughes (1983) has been studying the game of Four Square as played by girls in elementary school for four years, and has concluded that, while the game may be a nonliteral event (if you wish), the gaming that goes on around the game certainly is not. These girls play at manners while playing at the game. Their major dimension is that of nasty versus nice and they score the game by its fulfillment on this dimension rather than routinely by the game rules. Thus, if you put out a friend in a nice way, saying, for example, "Oh, I'm sorry, I didn't mean to throw so hard," the friend goes out. But if the friend can claim it was a nasty shot, the rest of the friends will support her in the illegitimacy of that shot. Unfortunately, even that statement is too simple because it transpires that whether your friends support you in the judgment of the shot depends, in turn, on your relationship to those friends. The judgment of nice or nasty is therefore dependent on the pre-existing sociometric structure or the pre-existing culture of peers. This means that in understanding a game we are involved in at least three terms: culture, gaming, and games. One remembers Whyte's (1933) work in which the gang's scores in bowling reproduced the linearity of the gang's sociometry. In that case there was not much "as if" at work. Most game-playing cultures are not as tightly knit, and the interrelationships of culture, gaming, and games can therefore be more variable. Still, the mere definition of play as as-if behavior is not sufficient; it all depends on which play and which context is being discussed.

Further, the as-if definition of play derives historically from the work of Schiller and Kant, for whom play is seen as a mediator between reason and perception (Spariosu, 1982). The as-if approach is, perhaps, also associated with romanticism and the decay of religious hegemony. In the past, the sense of otherness was most often an attribute of the sacred. As that concept has waned the sense of otherness has been attributed to more naturalistic sources, to sentiment, to the self, to esthetics, and, today, to play and even to sex.

If, on the other hand, we consider video games, the Krasnor and Pepler criteria of play appear to serve. The player must be very flexible in a nonliteral sphere; the affect is positive and excited and the motivation is certainly intrinsic. But video games are largely solitary activities and solitary play, as nursery play is, and they are clearly very different from what takes place among neighborhood groups in the streets. (However, when video games became so popular in the early 1980s many of the older populace declared them to be quite irrational forms of play leading to aggression, to addiction—and thence to gambling, it was said—to a perceptual-motor rigidity, to impulsive decision making, and to a generation of passive game players.)

Finally, we come to the most sanitized of all the modern research studies of play in the natural science tradition—the study of relationships between playing and problem solving. Here is rationality and the work ethic at its finest, based on the very solid ground that Köhler (1935) had already established: Even apes who play with sticks are better able to solve problems later with the same sticks. The rationality of play would certainly be well served if such a demonstration within a solid evolutionary paradigm could be brought to fruition.

Characteristically, in such studies, children are given ten or so minutes to manipulate freely the materials with which they will later have to solve problems, and are compared with others who have not had that play period or who have already been shown how to solve problems with such materials. One wonders, however, how many of us can perform in a strange environment with strange materials and strange people under the dictate to play. We might tentatively explore the materials, as Hutt (1979) has shown children first do with strange things in strange surroundings. But would we play? Fortunately, I don't have to examine this aberrant play tradition in detail because it has begun to self-destruct in the capable hands of its practitioners, including Pepler and Rubin (1982).

The import of this brief argument is that the constant turning away in our century from the study of play toward the study of its socialization correlates is not a mistake. It is rather a necessary part of a hegemonic cultural attitude that rationality, functionality, and work and industry and so on constitute what is important. It is also the related view that if play is to be redeemed it must make the right connections with socialization and maturity.

The larger question raised by this natural science tradition, however, is whether it is actually possible to study play with such methods. One possibility is that the problem is not intrinsic to natural science per se, only to the scientists' concern with socialization to the work ethic. This concern overwhelms the subject on behalf of all those other more valorized topics such as problem solving, playground apparatuses, preschool training programs, sex-role preferences, symbolic development, creativity, and reading. It could also be that natural science can not help because of its analytic-predictive mode of approach. Perhaps what is relatively less important about play is what is most predictable about it. Given that there is some management and educational value in knowing what to expect of the ages and of the sexes in terms of their probable play activities it might be argued that we have profited by our natural science research tradition. But this kind of tradition has told us very little about what play does for the players and has shown us little of how play does its idiosyncratic duty. One might assume that this kind of expression is more individualized than almost any other. It might, therefore, be much more helpful to have more descriptive records of players and their engagement over time with each other, with games, with their toys, and with playground apparatus.

Interpretive Science. If natural science findings have largely been a whitewash of our subject matter and have made more of fancy than of phantasmagoria, what of interpretive science? Has it served us any better? In a way, it has also served us a particular cultural dish, but the dish is more or less the obverse of that delivered by natural science.

Spariosu (1982) points out that the pre-Platonic view of play emphasizes to a very great extent the unpredictability of man's life on earth, and the way in which he is played fatefully by the gods. The Iliad is a war game among the gods, who are both free and irrational and who play with men like toys in some divine lottery. The gods themselves are like children who, at one moment, play with a doll and, at the next, dismember it to see what is inside. In Heraclitus, play as an arbitrary, spontaneous, and free movement becomes a philosophical principle for the first time. We should note, however, that this early idea of play as freedom implies that it is willful and dangerous, unlike many current definitions of play as freedom that seem to suggest only its spontaneity and rationality of choice.

It is not until Nietzsche (1974) in the second half of the nineteenth century that we once again hear a full statement of the earlier Homeric view of play as a species of irrationality—perhaps not surprisingly, given his generally power-oriented philosophy. Play is for him the exuberant Dionysian impulse beyond good and evil which wilfully engenders and destroys entire civilizations. For Nietzsche, the world is the play of eternal conflict—the basic kind of being in an ontological sense is irrational play. In his work, appearance, falsehood, fiction, representation, unreality, and irrationality become privileged terms and supplant such terms as essence, model truth, reality, and rationality which had been primary since Plato.

In general, people are so accustomed to thinking of play as a trivial, childlike, imitative, and secondary reality that it is almost impossible for us to grasp the view of ourselves as "played" by reality—the view of reality as a kind of playing. We are more inclined to think of play as a subcategory within sensible reality. Even when, like Freud, we suggest that irrationality as "primary process" is basic to human nature, we still see it as a subcategory within sensible reality. Even for

Freud, primary process seldom was the master; it was usually only the fractious servant in the house. In the more recent twentieth century phenomenological literature of Heidegger (1962), Gadamer (1982), and others, one also finds the idea that play is the basic mode of being, although in their cases, unlike Nietzsche's, higher metaphysical status is not accompanied by the same emphasis on irrationality. Unfortunately, like Nietzsche, they also talk about play in such global terms that it is very difficult for anyone trained in the natural science tradition of social science to feel much moved by the case. (A good example, or rather a bad example, of such diffuse use of the term is found in Hans, 1981.)

The part of the interpretive view of science which seems to me to have the greatest effect on play research has been developed by such leading figures as Turner, Goffman, and Geertz. These scholars are telling us about what things mean to those whom they study, and in all of their work there is, interestingly enough, a large debt to Nietzsche. Without exception, they assume that the play forms they observe are not just present in some essentialist Platonic way, but are forms of action used by the participants to achieve their ends. In Burke's (1979) sense, play is a part of the power politics of the groups in which it occurs.

Turner (1974), for example, sees play forms as an active technique by tribal members for resolving or assuaging social conflicts when other more direct forms are not available. Play expresses the orectic aspect of society as compared with its normative aspect; play forms are its antistructure, not its conventional structure. Society is divided within itself in a myriad of ways, and play forms enter into the political calculus of resolution and, occasionally, of change. In this dialectical approach, play's irrationality is regarded as a fundamental part of the social constitution. In such a framework we refer to play forms on a level that we can understand as festivals, sports, rituals, games, and so on. But in Turner we also receive the more abstract, metaphysical, and Nietzschean notion that society as a whole is a social drama which is played out in these and other ways. We are approaching the notion that reality is itself a form of playing.

Goffman (1959) also interprets small everyday situations through dramatistic and ludic metaphors. For him, members of society are constantly in rhetorical engagement for the maintenance of social equilibrium. Their plays are like those used on stage or those used in games. In holding such a view, Goffman has been accused by some of a cynical, manipulative view of society, and by others of showing the tremendous social interactive work and mutual respect that goes into the most minute of our social rituals, for example, walking down the street, talking over coffee, and playing games. Here again, however, we have the

Nietzschean view of society as a matter of the management of power, and we have play and games used as metaphors for illustrating that management. Whether Goffman's view is that life is a game or, rather, that it should be thought about metaphorically in game terms, is not quite clear. It certainly is the latter, but it may not be the former.

Finally, Geertz (1973) views society as a text to be read over the shoulders of the informants. In his case, "deep play" (for example, the Balinese cock fight) is merely one kind of text, although it is a text in which members intuit the deep social divisions of their own society and learn the political lessons of leaving evil alone. The predominant metaphor here is a narrative one, although in recently summing up the variety of humanistic metaphors now in operation within interpretive science, Geertz (1980) has suggested that the three major varieties— "life is a stage," "life is a game," and "life is a test"—are all metaphors of convenience for some larger target of scientific understanding. We are not simply possessed in some ludic universe.

Conclusion

In sum, while play has come to the fore as an idealized subject matter within natural science and has thus overcome some portion of its prior triviality and neglect (Fagen, 1980), it is still thought of largely as a rational, if inferior, form of human socialization. In interpretive science, on the other hand, play is seen as a more fundamental mode of the social structure, not simply a variation on individual behavior. Here, however, conceptions of the power of play's role in the politics of society vary from the clearly metaphoric interpretive usage of Geertz to the more ontological usage of Turner. In one conception, we may use our play for insight; in the other, we may be played with by the society of which we are a part.

I am bringing to the surface what a slippery position we are all in. The question is whose definition of play is the best context within which to study play. Is the natural science position the most valid? Which is the best assumption to make: the fiction that humans behave like determinate and rational physical matter, or the fiction that they have quite different humanistic modes of their own (ludic, dramatic, text)? Perhaps calling science a "fiction" is bothersome; perhaps I should speak of "paradigm" or "world hypothesis." But whatever term we use, it is reasonable to recognize that our presuppositions must be imagined before we can begin. So, not unreasonably, they might be called fictions or forms of play.

In this paper, I have attempted to address some of the larger and important philosophical, historical, and methodological issues in our current research in play. It should be clear that our current natural science research agendas bring recognition and even esteem to play but in a trivial and secondary fashion. Their concern is largely with rationality, socialization, and redemption. We are unwilling or reluctant to acknowledge that violent sports, libidinous foreplay, addictive gambling, strategic war games, video games, "seven minutes in heaven," Little League baseball, Barbie doll play, playing house, playing with toy trucks, and with mobiles hanging over a crib are all part of the necessary subject matter of play that we must deal with. Furthermore, we must also tackle the use of some or all of these phenomena as a source of metaphors for other life activities that are employed by social scientists, by philosophers, and, today, by politicians and everyone else. How is it that play and game concepts are increasingly taking the place of earlier religious and evolutionary concepts for describing human affairs and our place in the world?

In these terms, then, games are neither inherently rational or irrational. They can be both. Similarly the freedom of play can be blessed or cursed. It can be the freedom of the dilettante or of the obsessed. Again, the otherness or as-if nature of play and games can be the fantasy of Alice in Wonderland or the demoniacal possession of professional football. The activities of the players can be a contest, a representation, or a transformation. Play can be competitive or cooperative. It can be the ultimate reality or the ultimate unreality.

Whatever it is, enough has been said to underline that the two major empirical traditions of this century have each absorbed into their presuppositions different views of play which have served to context the texts they choose to study. In the case of imaginative play, the natural science view has rendered it relatively rational and insipid, while the interpretive science view has rendered it relatively irrational and nefarious. The three papers under discussion vary along just such a continuum of rationality-irrationality, insipidity-nefariousness.

Personal Epilogue. If it seems that I am attempting to have it both ways, or neither way, that is in fact the case. I serve as a psychologist in a program in human learning and development within a graduate school of education, and also as a folklorist in a department of folklore within a faculty of arts and sciences. In the former setting I deal daily with faculty and students who believe that the world is a scientifically determinable place; that it has laws; that these are observable, predictable, and verifiable; that even the human world can be seen as behavior and as an object for study; and that the contexts or texts must be seen as phenomena which are physically specifiable and controllable in some explicit sense, or can at least be categorized as simple-complex, barren-cluttered, and so on. Attempts to give a more adequate interpretation of what is transpiring—by entering into relationships with subjects which will reveal the subtlety of the meanings involved—are usually rejected as too subjective, anecdotal, open-ended, or even illusory.

The positive side of this tradition is its accomplishments in many areas of social science, including those of consumer prediction, cognitive development, physiological psychology, and psychometric assessment, among others. The negative side is the blind devotion to experimental method or behavioral method—thousands upon thousands of results are either nugatory or predict such small amounts of the variance (albeit in a statistically significant way) that the studies become exercises in the methodological ritual rather than credible contributions to any powerful conception of human lawfulness. My direct experience, as mentioned earlier, has been with play research and also with studies of sibling differences which, in a recent review, I have characterized as a thousand studies of low-level correlations between this-or-that sibling position and other measures all in search of an interpretation (Lamb and Sutton-Smith, 1982). Because there has been so little anthropological study of the sibling phenomenon itself, these correlational and experimental studies, while replete with results, some of which are occasionally consistent, await adequate interpretation. In general, the speculative nature of the conclusion or discussion sections of most of the articles in the psychological literature is not at all scientific in the same sense that the methodological sections are scientific. It is as if the laws of nature thus assessed are supposed to speak for themselves; such is the naive philosophical realism presupposed in most of these studies. But nature does not speak for itself; it must be interpreted.

By contrast, in the folklore department of which I am also a member the concern of the members is precisely interpretation—historical, literary, anthropological, esthetic, philosophical, and ethnographic. Instead of assuming that the human world is a given and lawful proposition, most folklorists assume that it is an intricate, multilaminated, ongoing, partly ritualistic, and partly openended sequence of events which is seldom easily captured, no matter what methodology is used. There is often a sophistication about the conception of human reality involved in the study of folklore which makes the routine examinations we are familiar with in developmental psychology seem beggarly by comparison. On the other hand, when life is seen as such a flux, efforts to provide verifiable conclusions about it are often primitive as compared with those to be found in developmental psychology. In this light one might contrast the complex, relatively nonrigorous account of riddles offered by McDowell (1979), the folklorist, with the relatively simple but relatively rigorous account of the difference between play and exploration offered by Hutt (1979). They are both excellent examples of their kind of investigation and both make important contributions to our knowledge of children's play.

Similarly, I find the quite different approaches of the investigators included in this volume all rewarding in different ways. Although the contributions of Göncü and Kessel and Forbes and Yablick are relatively rigorous, they have nevertheless adventured into newer and subtler areas of meaning in children's play, and the outcomes are richer than usual for developmental studies of children's play. In turn, because of its openendedness, the chapter by Kelly-Byrne gives us a multi-textured account of text and context replete with, and approaching in its suggestiveness at least, some of the probable complexity of true human interaction. What the account lacks in natural science rigor, it gains in its courageous attempt to reckon with interpretive human complexity. What it lacks in -etics it gains in -emics.

Finally, it will also be clear from my earlier historical analysis that while I am encouraged by the way in which the issue of text and context has brought this controversy between natural and interpretive science to the doorstep of ludic studies, I do not regard either natural or interpretive science as anything more than partial attempts at ludic epistemology. We stand at the threshold of an intrusion into social science by modes once known as purely or largely literary, esthetic, or ludic. I believe the subtlety of novelists and players will be an ever-increasing challenge and threat to the tedium and triviality of our science.

References

Bamberg, M. "Metaphor and Play Interaction in Young Children." In F. E. Manning (Ed.), *The World of Play*. West Point, N.Y.: Leisure Press, 1983.
Bateson, G. *Steps to an Ecology of Mind*. New York: Ballantine, 1972.
Bernstein, R. J. *The Restructuring of Social and Political Theory*. Philadelphia: University of Pennsylvania Press, 1978.
Burke, K. *A Grammar of Motives*. (2nd ed.) Berkeley: University of California Press, 1969 [1945].
Burke, K. *Language as Symbolic Action*. Berkeley: University of California Press, 1974.
Corsaro, W. "'We're Friends Right?' Children's Use of Access Rituals in Nursery School." *Language in Society*, 1979, *8* (3), 315-336.
Fagen, R. *Animal Play Behavior*. New York: Oxford University Press, 1980.
Gadamer, H. G. *Truth and Method*. New York: Crossroad, 1982.
Geertz, C. *The Interpretation of Cultures*. New York: Basic Books, 1973.
Geertz, C. "Blurred Genres: The Refiguration of Social Thought." *The American Scholar*, 1980, *49* (2), 165-179.

Goffman, E. *The Presentation of Self in Everyday Life.* New York: Doubleday, 1959.
Hall, E. *The Hidden Dimension.* Garden City, N.J.: Anchor Books, 1969.
Hans, J. S. *The Play of the World.* Amherst: University of Massachusetts, 1981.
Heidegger, M. *Being and Time.* New York: Harper & Row, 1962.
Hughes, L. A. "Beyond the Rules of the Game: Why Are Rooie Rules Nice?" In F. E. Manning (Ed.), *The World of Play.* West Point, N.Y.: Leisure Press, 1983.
Hutt, C. "Exploration and Play." In B. Sutton-Smith (Ed.), *Play and Learning.* New York: Gardner Press, 1979.
Jones, B., and Hawes, B. *Step on Down.* New York: Harper & Row, 1972.
Knapp, M., and Knapp, H. *One Potato, Two Potato.* New York: Norton, 1976.
Köhler, W. *The Mentality of Apes.* New York: Harcourt Brace Jovanovich, 1935.
Krasnor, L. R., and Pepler, D. J. "The Study of Children's Play: Some Suggested Future Directions." In K. Rubin (Ed.), *Children's Play.* New Directions for Child Development, no. 9. San Francisco: Jossey-Bass, 1980.
Lamb, M., and Sutton-Smith, B. (Eds.). *Sibling Relationships: Their Nature and Significance Across the Life Span.* Hillsdale, N.J.: Erlbaum, 1982.
McDowell, J. *Children's Riddling.* Bloomington, Ind.: University of Indiana Press, 1979.
Nietzsche, F. *The Birth of Tragedy and the Case of Wagner.* New York: Random House, 1974.
Opie, I., and Opie, P. *The Lore and Language of School Children.* New York: Oxford University Press, 1968.
Pepler, D. J., and Rubin, K. (Eds.). "The Play of Children: Current Theory and Research." *Contributions to Human Development,* 1982, 6.
Sluckin, A. *Growing Up in the Playground.* London: Routledge & Kegan Paul, 1982.
Spariosu, M. (Ed.). *Literature, Mimesis and Play.* Tubingen, W. Germany: Gunter Narr Verlag, 1982.
Sutton-Smith, B. "A Formal Analysis of Game Meaning." *Western Folklore,* 1959, *18* (1), 13–24.
Sutton-Smith, B. *A History of Children's Play.* Philadelphia: University of Pennsylvania Press, 1981.
Sutton-Smith, B., and Kelly-Byrne, D. *The Masks of Play.* West Point, N.Y.: Leisure Press, 1984a.
Sutton-Smith, B., and Kelly-Byrne, D. "The Idealization of Play." In D. K. Smith (Ed.), *Play in Animals and Humans.* London: Van Nostrand, 1984b.
Turner, V. *Dramas, Fields, and Metaphors.* Ithaca, N.Y.: Cornell University Press, 1974.
Whyte, W. F. *Streetcorner Society.* Chicago: University of Chicago Press, 1933.

Brian Sutton-Smith is professor of education and director of the Program in Human Learning and Development at the University of Pennsylvania. He received his doctorate from the University of New Zealand in 1955 and is the author of many books in the areas of play and social development.

By taking a natural science perspective, it is possible to think about different ways of understanding this curious behavior — play — and to think of different ways of probing the phenomenon to determine whether it will behave as expected.

New Wine in Old Bottles

Greta Fein

The analysis of children's play has contributed in several ways to the study of human development. First, in contrast to notions of developmental problems as the study of children's solutions to experimenter-designed tasks, play research offers notions of how children manage the intricate behavior they design for themselves. Because play, like speech or social interaction, is a multilayered human activity, the attempt to understand it will necessarily encourage a variety of theoretical perspectives. Of these, no single one will initially embrace more than a small part of the larger phenomenon. One marvelous aspect of play research, richly demonstrated in this collection of studies, is that diverse theoretical contexts can be used to interpret play episodes. In these studies, the investigators have asked some very different questions: "Suppose we liken play to a system of communication?" "Suppose we liken play to a dramatic presentation?" "A religious text?" Each likening promises new hunches about the phenomenon, hunches that amount to informed guesses about its structure and function. Some of these hunches will make more sense than others; some will continue to make sense after they have been elaborated, extended, and tested. At some point, these newly made theoretical containers — with older ones borrowed from Mead, Piaget, Freud, or Vygotsky (to name but a few) — will surely be replaced by more inclusive and powerful conceptualizations. Someday we may have sturdy new bottles for our sparkling wine. It is important to welcome diverse and innovative constructions and recognize at the same time that the process of general theory construction in imaginative play is in its early stages.

Second, the stress on child-managed behavior demands a methodology minimally invaded by adult intrusions. Therefore, investigators interested in the study of play typically observe children in naturalistic settings, or in laboratory playrooms designed to look like naturalistic settings. Of course, the term *naturalistic* is a red flag. Whether the setting is a preschool, a bedroom, a playground, a beach, or a forest; whether the child is alone, with peers, or with adults, settings are touched in numerous and different ways both by the notions of adults (parents, teachers, priests, and police), of what should or should not occur, and by children's notions of what these adult notions are (Fein, 1983; King, 1979). The studies described in this volume are conducted in settings that were more or less familiar to the children, containing either adult or peer companions, presenting more or less ambiguous adult roles, and involving an adult presence more or less explicit with respect to the organization of material things and social rules.

Settings in their subtlety and diversity certainly merit study, since any grand theory of play will have to explain how features of settings are incorporated in the play, how they modify it, and how they are variously perceived by the players. While peculiar, unusual, or bizarre settings probably require special consideration, I think it is a mistake to argue about the settings in which "pure" play, or "real" play occurs. Settings, as a given collection of movable or fixed, ignorable or captivating parts, are as much psychological contexts as are the context-setting behaviors people use to manipulate their own and others' behavior. In interesting but different ways, some aspects of the setting are neglected in these studies while others receive attention. In the analyses presented by Göncü and Kessel in Chapter One, aspects of the setting are incorporated into the coding of conversation, while in those offered by Kelly-Byrne in Chapter Three places such as bedrooms and backyards are incorporated into the general interpretation. And yet this information that is used implicitly would be illuminating if it were made explicit. Bedrooms and backyards contain features such as messy or immaculate, small or spacious, and barren or cluttered that tell much about their owners and, perhaps, about what behavior is welcomed, expected, or accepted in such settings.

Third, play investigators have had the courage to use controlled laboratory designs as well as observational procedures, and often the same investigator will use both procedures in the same study (for example, Watson and Fischer, 1980). Depending on the question, it may be useful to add or eliminate one or more factors responsible for a given aspect of behavior. It is likely, for example, that young children comprehend the meaning of transformation statements before they produce them; if only peer play is observed, productive rather than receptive competence will be studied. The studies in this volume, each in its own way, imposed some control over the children's behavior—by using a standard playroom, familiar peer groups of fixed size and sex, or by eliminating peers entirely and providing a single, unfamiliar adult. Interestingly, the study presented as the most processual (Kelly-Byrne) illustrates the most extreme reduction insofar as it occurs in a home stripped of parents, relatives, friends, television, and telephone.

Finally, play research has historically drawn key images from clinical, case study, impressionistic, and even anecdotal material. Piaget (1962) describes his children's play alone and with others—but in order to grasp Piaget's interpretation one must read the transcript and let the scope of the theoretical ideas sink in. Erikson (1977), Gould (1972), and Hartley and others (1952)—our eminent baby biographers (see Darwin, 1877)—and countless others have contributed in diverse ways to the collective qualitative data base upon which contemporary research builds. An interest in formal classification and quantification, though relatively recent, appeared after a fairly long period of qualitative incubation. Rigorously defined classification strategies for quantifying play behavior are still in an early stage. Which strategies will yield the greatest insights is yet to be determined; the outcome will depend, in part, on the nomological networks these insights produce.

The shift from speculative to empirical and from qualitative to quantitative requires an enormous investment of time, patience, and dedication. The analyses reported in this volume by Göncü and Kessel and by Forbes and Yablick (Chapter Two) describe only a small portion of the data collected by the investigators, first steps in a long process of data reduction and data analysis. The important point, however, is that these efforts at classification and quantification were inspired by ideas of what play might mean to the participants. The next step, an even more arduous one, is to construct formal and abstract representations of the structure of this meaning and how it operates. Notions of metacommunication, transformation, and coherence imply rule-governed behavior. But in play, these rules must refer to general play "policies" with more flexible "executive" rules postulated at a lower level to deal with moment-to-moment shifts and negotiations.

Issues Related to Context

The issue of text and context complicates an already complicated problem. These studies nicely illustrate some of the positions one might adopt in exploring the figure-ground relations of play. Four specific problem areas that emerge from these studies merit special consideration.

Context as Temporal or Concurrent Relationships. Two chapters illustrate a view of context as relations that unfold over time. Göncü and Kessel mark time into discrete segments marking the initiation, maintenance, and termination of play. Metacommunications (behaviors such as invitations, transformations, and plans that express contextual information) will presumably exhibit different forms when they are used to initiate, maintain, or terminate an episode. This view of context generates some interesting and testable hypotheses. One might propose, for example, that invitations will occur at the beginning of an episode, while transformations and plans occur later on. I suspect that this hypothesis will be only partially confirmed; transformations are probably free-floating, flexible moves that invite and announce as well as maintain and extend dramatic play. If a temporal model is pursued further, one can ask more refined questions about temporal contingencies among these statements; and when two children are involved, it might be illuminating to compare individual metaprofiles.

Kelly-Byrne's study also adopts the view that context is temporally organized: While the present is understood in terms of the past ("before" is the context of "now"), the present can precipitate a reinterpretation of the past ("now" is the context of "before"), which then becomes a "new before" with which to interpret the "next now." Although timebound, this model is nonlinear. It also illustrates a functional approach to context, in which context depends on how material is used, rather than on what it is. Context is active, while text is passive; context, which absorbs text, is the primary datum for inferring text. The absorption position is so salient in this view that we seem to be left with temporally shifting con(text)s rather than the fairly autonomous text and context assumed by Göncü and Kessel.

If Kelly-Byrne absorbs text into context, Forbes and Yablick move in the opposite direction. In their analyses, the dramatic presentation is the text, while the real world designated in the drama is the context. Adopting the position that play is a window, these investigators argue that understanding how children bring coherence to their dramatic presentations will illuminate how they bring coherence to their real-world experience. In this study, the dramatic text is used to infer context. Because the real world, stored as "scripts," guides the organization of text (Schank and Abelson, 1977), Forbes and Yablick seem to view the temporal relation between these elements as concurrent rather than sequential.

Reality and Pretense. Interestingly, these papers also illustrate different stances with respect to the meaning of reality and the meaning of pretense. For Göncü and Kessel, the issue poses few problems; the pretend play of children is taken at its face value, and the investigators attempt to capture as accurately as possible the children's expressed play transformations—pretense is what the children consider it to be.

For Kelly-Byrne, in her chapter in this volume, the distinction is painful and difficult. This investigator adopts the view that "... participants create reality through their own constructions... all meaning is seen to be intersubjective and emergent... " (p. 37). Consider the study: Diana, a researcher, plays the role of babysitter for Helen, a lonely, precocious seven-year-old. The burden on Diana is enormous; she first must pretend to be a babysitter, then pretend to be a play partner, knowing that tapes of what transpires will need to be enriched by field notes recording other aspects of the encounter. The reader easily empathizes with Helen's efforts to penetrate Diana's compliant, measured demeanor: have we here a babysitter, a teenager, a reincarnated mother, or, perhaps, Wonder Woman? Schwartzman's (1978) criticism of ethological studies in which the researchers "pretend they do not exist" (p. 314) seems to apply as well to participant-observer studies in which the researchers pretend to be that which they are not.

These issues bear upon the claims of the study as well as its title. It is appropriate to ask whether Helen and Diana created a common reality through their own constructions and whether these two created anything but the most superficial intersubjective meaning. The relationship more often resembles that of patient-therapist than that of mutually invested play partners. As the title of Kelly-Byrne's chapter suggests, the fabling came not only from Helen; it seemed rather to penetrate the relationship at many levels, beginning with Diana's vague reference to her work at the university. Regardless of phenomenological rhetoric, meaning in this study is given by an investigator to the investigator's construction of the subject's reality. As in much behavioral research, one participant (the scientist) controls the setting (as well as the measurement), and ultimately defines the other's constructions and meanings from a vantage point presumably detached from the relationship. Most certainly, in this study the detachment is complicated by the investigator's self-perceptions and reactions to the long fourteen-month encounter, perceptions and reactions which are conspicuously missing from the record. Can there be intersubjective meaning in the absence of intrasubjective awareness?

Forbes and Yablick call upon "scripts" as the reality reference of dramatic play. According to Schank and Abelson (1977), scripts are cognitive structures that store information about everyday activities.

The activities are life's well-learned, dull, automated routines; scripts store the nitty details of the sequences in which these routines are carried out. Forbes and Yablick suggest that the symbol systems of social interaction might come from general scripts of human action, that is, at some level the relation between drama and script is literal. If so, the study of pretending will illuminate children's real-life knowledge; a thesaurus of make-believe would provide a compendium of children's knowledge about familiar routines and social occasions.

This notion runs into trouble at several junctures. Consider, for example, the idea that pretense becomes increasingly coherent as measured by the ratios suggested by Burke (1969). However, if as Forbes and Yablick demonstrate in their chapter in this sourcebook, some ratios show a decrease from five to seven years of age (scene/behavior, behavior/behaivor, scene/character; see Figure 1, p. 29), does this mean that coherence diminishes with age? While coherence is a powerful idea, the problem appears to be one of clarifying the measurement continuum: What does zero mean? Another, more general problem is whether children's dramatic scenarios—either in theme or in behavioral sequencing—resemble the stereotyped, mundane behavior coded in scripts. With respect to theme, the answer given in the transcripts provided in all three studies here appears to be no. Play scenarios do not deal with fundamental action sequences known by all children such as toileting, dressing, crayoning, and so on. Rather, the themes most often are rare or special occasions (weddings, company, and restaurants) in which the key characters are either adults or younger children, or fictitious television or story characters (dinosaurs, Superman, and Wonder Woman). Mundane activities, if included at all, are often expressed as abbreviated, exaggerated, and salient moments capturing the essence of a particular activity, rather than its details. For example, pretending to wash dishes is abbreviated as the transfer of clattering pots, plates, and utensils in and out of the sink accompanied by rubbing gestures; cooking dinner is shown by stirring and pouring from pots equally likely to be full or empty; and even serving a meal rarely involves sequenced activities such as setting the table, serving, eating, and cleaning up. Although the general outline of real-life sequences may be preserved (Fenson and Ramsay, 1981), the level of detail implied by script theory is rarely rendered in children's spontaneous play (Genishi, 1983). If these pretending four-year-olds were asked to wash real dishes with real soap and water, would they demonstrate adult knowledge of the details? In what ways would the elements and sequences of real washing and play washing differ?

An alternative view to the one proposed by Forbes and Yablick stresses that pretense reflects physical and social knowledge under construction — crude and fuzzy knowledge that in adulthood might be stored as scripts. If one were to make a compendium of imaginative play themes, one might have an interesting collection of what children find problematic, curious, and even disturbing. The scheme for classifying dramatic elements proposed by these authors might then be expanded to include the themes rendered by the children. Such a scheme would yield a theme-by-element topology revealing how physical and social meaning (not the real world) is constructed. Unfortunately, however, the thematic content of imagined play in play research has thus far received less attention than it merits. (See Garvey, 1977, Chapter Six, and Sutton-Smith and others, 1978, for potentially useful ways of analyzing play themes.)

Context as Verbal Behavior. Studies of play typically differ with respect to their emphasis on verbal communication; the studies included in this volume are no exception. Forbes and Yablick consider only utterances; Göncü and Kessel (1984) have coded nonverbal matieral, but the analyses presented here consider only that which is spoken; Kelly-Byrne uses both verbal and nonverbal information. Although this is a controversial issue (McLoyd, 1982), it is unlikely that children's understanding and negotiation of play scenarios can be penetrated if nonverbal communication is excluded from the analysis.

A good example of the problem is presented in Göncü and Kessel's transcript of the wedding-dance scene in Chapter One of this volume. As verbal exchange, the speech seems strikingly egocentric — R. talks about a wedding, calls the wedding man, and then asks, "Who is going to marry me?" (I assume that she is looking at A. as she poses the question). A. rejects R.'s proposal (although it is not clear whether she is also rejecting the role of groom), and placing the tie on the rack, proposes a dance as an alternative. When, however, one considers the props, the scene makes more sense, although the egocentrism of the children becomes more striking. Oblivious to her tutu (dance), R. attends to her flowers (wedding), and A.'s tie (male role). By contrast A. sees the tutu (dance), ignores the flowers until brought to her attention by R., and puts the tie back as she realizes where the conversation is going. When A. reviews the possibilities she makes it clear that both girls will marry, but not one another, and the dance is incorporated into the wedding. But the meaning of the flowers remains unnegotiated, and eventually this lack of shared meaning disrupts the play.

Admittedly, the above interpretation will be difficult to code, and I cringe at the thought of reaching agreement on interpretation itself.

However, if verbally expressed prop transformations encourage negotiation and the creation of shared meaning, one might argue that episodes lacking these transformation statements will be brief (eleven rounds in this transcript) compared with episodes in which these statements are plentiful. If we added a measure of the number of theme-relevant props (in this case, seven—tutu, flowers, tie, broom, purse, shoes, and phone), we can note that only one is explicitly referred to (a low ratio of transformations to things). Perhaps, then, episodes will be quickly aborted when children fail to make explicit reference to props that are relevant to the play. Analyses of this type deal with the "invisible" information discussed by Kelly-Byrne. If it can be shown that things not talked about influence the flow of play, the effort to find more direct ways of identifying this "invisible" information might prove fruitful. The interesting problem is that while this information is literally visible to both the participants and the observer, it is difficult to represent concretely in the analytical framework.

Text as Representation or Presentation. Play is typically viewed as a mode of symbolic representation in which connected expressive acts convey roles, feelings, situation, and relationships. Play as representation considers the players' involvement in acts that simulate states, persons, concerns, situations, and so on (Burke's pentad, and more [Burke, 1969]). In rendering these representations, children swish hips, speak sternly, raise eyebrows, and even slump. The study of play as representation requires attention to these gestures, expressions, and postures as well as to verbal utterances, to thematic content, and to dramatic forms or verbal discourse.

These studies present a somewhat different view, one in which play emerges as presentation rather than representation. Although the specific approaches differ, the central concern often seems to be the narrative story, its coherence, or its communicability. One implication of play metacommunications—an implication that is even stronger in the dramatist perspective—is that children scrutinize their own and their partner's behavior, holding this behavior to the standard of a critical audience judging the quality of the production. Presentational play might mark the beginnings of conscious awareness that personal action is something to think about, produce, change, and evaluate in relation to the actions of others. If so, the distinction between play as representation and play as presentation is of considerable theoretical importance. Play of young children is more likely to be representational— more concerned with expressiveness than with story line. By ages five to seven, children switch to more narrative presentations.

Göncü and Kessel have transcribed their data in a form that

makes possible an analysis of the relation between representation and presentation. The dramatist scheme used by Forbes and Yablick is intriguing because it may also reveal components of this awareness. In their attention to the children's tendency to reject or accept (implicitly or explicitly) an imagined proposal, both teams of investigators touch the issue of a reflective self and awareness of others. However, something other than a mean difference model of analysis will be needed to display these developmental sequences.

New Wine: Rational Science and Irrational Events

The research reported in these chapters departs from the past in important and provocative ways. Children's play, especially play dealing with symbolic materials, provides mysteries of purpose, organization, and consequence that are far from being solved. I am impressed by these studies because they explore new ways in which we as observers can think about the meaning of imaginative play. Further, the chapters provoke controversies about the most useful stance to take with respect to the meaning of science, the study of human consciousness, and the role of context and imaginative play in an analysis of human development (particularly Sutton-Smith's contribution, Chapter Four.) Two studies (Göncü and Kessel, Forbes and Yablick) are cast within the perspective of natural science; the third (Kelly-Byrne) adopts an interpretive science perspective.

One general issue is whether the assumptions and methods of natural science are adequate to the task of understanding imaginative play. Before this issue is approached, we need to be clear about what we mean by natural science and what we hope to achieve by the study of imaginative play. Philosophers of science have come to distinguish between general models of scientific activity, and how practicing scientists think about both what they do, and what they seem indeed to do (Kuhn, 1962; Polanyi, 1946). Yet, even as philosophers debate the foundations of natural science, the meaning of objectivity, and assumptions about a real world, scientific achievements of immense significance continue to be made, as if the enterprise itself were unperturbed by philosophical dilemmas. These achievements, no longer limited to the inanimate world, now include startling notions about the origin, functioning and replication of living systems, abstract notions responsible for the all-too-real practicalities of genetic engineering.

In any event, it is apparent that science involves conceptual tools (such as making inferences from the observed to the unobserved, or the elaboration of generative deductive systems) as well as methodological ones. Methodological devices (such as empirical verification, reproducibility of results, agreement between measures using different and independent methods, and confirmation of predictions) continue to be powerful and useful. Yet these devices are surely not infallible formulas for scientific success. Even powerful tools will be useless in the absence of what Polanyi (1946) refers to as the "fundamental guesses of science concerning the nature of things" (p. 28) and of the scientist's sustaining belief that there is something there that can be understood. The scientific task includes ". . . the finding of a good problem, . . . the surmises to pursue it, and the recognition of a discovery that solves it" (p. 15). The sense of a problem is crucial: "Either you know what you are looking for and then there is no problem; or you do not know what you are looking for, and then you are not looking for anything and cannot expect to find it" (p. 14).

Polanyi's story of the burglar in the house succinctly expresses one scientist's view of the scientific perspective. Suppose you are wakened one night by a noise in an empty room in your house: "Is it the wind? A burglar? A rat? We try to guess. Was that a footfall? That means a burglar! Convinced, we pluck up courage, rise, and proceed to verify our assumption" (p. 23). The observer's state of consciousness is assumed to be wakeful; the room, the footsteps, and the burglar are assumed to be real entities. The assertion concerning the burglar is viewed as a proposition about something real and open to verification by some definite, although perhaps as-yet-undefined operations. Our burglar-investigating scientist might make a call to the police, or grab a flashlight or a weapon before making his observation. The system works because the scientist has constructed a set of relevant categories and knows something about the properties of wind, rats, and footfalls, the kinds of things likely to make noises in the night. Because science is a systematic and cumulative body of knowledge, the scientist's categories and ways of looking are taken from the past (both personal and cultural). Further, if there is no burglar, no wind, and no rat, other clues might be sought and new possibilities considered; if need be, "whumps" might be invented to account for the phenomenon.

Taking a natural science perspective, I can liken play to Polanyi's burglar. I can think about different ways of understanding this curious behavior and of different ways of probing the phenomenon to determine whether it will behave the way I think it will. I can think of play as real, as I can think of categories such as transformations, agent, and scene as real, even though I recognize that these categories come from the intellectual culture in which I have been educated. The process is similar to what Hofstadter (1979) calls a "strange loop." I can really pretend that something I am inventing is real. I am concious of the as-if status of ideas that I believe might describe the reality of consciousness itself.

It seems fair to ask how a hermeneutic scientist might respond to noises in the night. Clues to general features of this response are provided by Manicas and Secord (1983) who, while granting that natural science methods are needed to investigate the abstract properties of physical, biological, and psychological entities, claim that they cannot explain or predict real-life phenomena—a particular volcano, historical episode, or human individual. In psychology, according to these authors, hermeneutic science involves an effort to understand "the concrete person and his or her life history and particular patterns of behavior, including, as reflectively applied, self-understanding" (p. 411). This approach is biographical, involving a sustained effort to "grasp the person's meanings and understandings... vision of the world, his or her plans, purposes, motivations, and interests" (p. 409). Were one to adopt this approach, which resembles a traditional clinical study, insights about play would be incidental to the main purpose of understanding a particular individual.

A somewhat different view is offered by Schwartzman (1978) who recorded the activities of a particular playgroup in a daycare center. This study was not about concrete individuals in the sense meant by Manicas and Secord; rather, the unit of analysis was a group whose history, patterns of behavior, visions, plans, or purposes are not the same as those of the individuals who make up the group. Are the relevant observations, then, only those activities in which all members of the group are involved? In order to understand the group, is it necessary to observe the group in circumstances other than play? If, however, play is the unit of analysis, the group might be flexibly defined and nonplay activities eliminated. What is the unit of analysis—the group, or the play episode? Is the group the context of the play, or is play the context of the group? An easy answer seems to be "both," which in the natural science perspective would mean "the play of the group." However, because this formulation implies two layers of abstraction, it lacks the concreteness assumed by hermeneutic science; can we liken this group of children to the Balinese and can we liken their play to a stable cultural form such as a cockfight? (See Schwartzman, 1978; Sutton-Smith in this volume for discussion of Geertz's (1972) study of the Balinese cockfight and its relevance to the study of play.)

Returning to our burglar, would a hermeneutic scientist set out to study the empty room? The house? Or, perhaps, the noise-hearing scientist? If the noise were outdoors, what would be the natural unit of analysis? At the very least, the hermeneutic effort seems to require a clear, unambiguous, and concrete entity—stable, well-formed, and worthy of in-depth study. Ironically, this fluid, changing, and meaning-laden abstraction called play may be the wrong subject to study with hermeneutic devices. In setting out to study a fluid, shifting, and open system as if it were a stable, closed society or a traditional cultural form, one is likely to end up studying either nothing or, at best, one's own unacknowledged presuppositions about something.

Polanyi's burglar simplifies considerably the role of the observer. One basis for the criticism of the notion of an objective, detached scientist comes from quantum theorists who view the observer as an essential component of the definition of an event. Imagine that there is indeed a burglar in Polanyi's empty room. Imagine that there is also a jar of lethal gas over which a trip hammer is suspended. The hammer is activated by a counter that records random events and the system is set so that there is a probability of one-half that the hammer will be released. In quantum mechanics the system is represented mathematically as the sum of a live burglar and a dead burglar function. The first question is whether Polanyi's burglar is alive or dead. Before the observer looks in the room both possibilities are equally likely; once the measurement is taken the burglar is either dead or alive (Morowitz, 1980). Until a measurement is made the observer cannot know what state the system is in. If the burglar is dead, the second question is, Who killed him? Measurement, which in this theory constitutes an event, involves an observer who becomes aware of an empirical outcome. Moreover, there are consequences to the observer's behavior because the active measurement throws the system into one state or another (Hofstadter and Dennett, 1981).

In spite of the implications of modern physics for the study of human beings, it offers no justification for the observer-as-participant view. In the quantum mechanics model, on the contrary, once the observer enters the room we have a live-observer and a live-observer function, subject to measurement by an observer outside the room. Quantum theory does indirectly have a message bearing upon the issue posed by Sutton-Smith—whether play as a presumably irrational activity can be rationally conceptualized. Interestingly, Einstein objected to quantum theory because, as he explained, God does not play dice. Quantum theory seems to illustrate a case in which the rational tools of science and mathematics lead coolly to conceptions of the universe as irrational. There seems to be no reason, at least in principle, why a phenomenon presumed to be irrational (play) should be beyond the bounds of rational science even if we view play as a generator of random events.

There are numerous other implications of quantum theory worthy of contemplation. Consider, for example, the epistemological circle this theory presents to reductionist theories of mind. Suppose we hold that reflective thought and consciousness can be explained by activities of the nervous system which can be understood by biological mechanisms at the next lower level. These in turn can be understood in terms of atomic physics — the actions of atoms of carbon, nitrogen, oxygen, and other elements. However, atomic physics is now best understood by means of quantum mechanics which is formulated with human consciousness as a primitive component of the system (Morowitz, 1980). The notion that understanding a phenomenon involves levels of nested structures representing different systems is attractive (Bronfenbrenner, 1977), but the resulting scheme is neither holistic nor reductionist insofar as it permits upward causality as well as downward causality, and "upstream" events as well as "downstream" events.

The general problem of understanding human consciousness, especially the possibilities of downward and upward causality, has been brilliantly explored by Dennett (1978), Hofstadter (1979), and Hofstadter and Dennett (1981). The importance of this discussion relates directly to the question of text and context insofar as understanding at one level may provide a context for understanding either a higher or a lower level; any particular conceptual orientation can function as either text or context, depending on whether one is moving upstream or downstream. To return to the studies reported in this volume, the age of a play participant (viewed as a biological factor) or the role of entities such as scripts (viewed as programs coded in neural networks) can be thought of as upsteam constructs, while anthropological notions about culture or sociological notions about institutions can be thought of as downstream constructs. In an important sense context or text depends on the measurement — on the observer's consciousness — and not on the emergent meaning of the participant. (While we can think about the mind of the live burglar, it is harder to think about the mind of the dead one.)

The matter of human consciousness is relevant to play for several reasons. Because the transformational aspects of play involve a conjunction of the literal and the nonliteral, and because these transformations involve recursive thinking — thinking about a reflecting self in relation to other reflecting selves relating to nonreflecting inanimate objects — the study of symbolic play might yield insights about the origins of the mind's ability to manage seminal "strange loops." We find "strange loops" abundantly in this remarkable childhood activity.

References

Bronfenbrenner, U. *The Ecology of Human Development.* Cambridge, Mass.: Harvard University Press, 1977.
Burke, K. *A Grammar of Motives.* (2nd ed.) Berkeley: University of California Press, 1969 [1945].
Darwin, C. "A Biographical Sketch of an Infant." *Mind,* 1877, *2,* 286–294.
Dennett, D. C. *Brainstorms.* Montgomery, Vt.: Bradford Books, 1978.
Erikson, E. H. *Toys and Reasons.* New York: Norton, 1977.
Fein, G. G. "Learning in Play: Surfaces of Thinking and Feeling." Paper presented at the International Conference on Play and Play Environments, Austin, Texas, July 1983.
Fenson, L., and Ramsay, D. S. "Effects of Modeling Action Sequences on the Play of Twelve-, Fifteen-, and Nineteen-Month-Old Children." *Child Development,* 1981, *52* (3), 1028–1036.
Garvey, C. *Play.* Cambridge, Mass.: Harvard University Press, 1977.
Geertz, C. "The Play: Notes on the Balinese Cockfight." *Daedalus,* 1972, *101,* 1–38.
Genishi, C. "Role Initiation in the Discourse of Mexican-American Children's Play." Paper presented at the annual meeting of the American Educational Research Association, Montreal, 1983.
Göncü, A., and Kessel, F. Personal communication, 1984.
Gould, R. *Child Studies Through Fantasy.* New York: Quadrangle, 1972.
Hartley, R. E., Frank, L. K., and Goldenson, R. M. *Understanding Children's Play.* New York: Columbia University Press, 1952.
Hofstadter, D. R. *Gödel, Escher, Bach: An Eternal Golden Braid.* New York: Vintage Books, 1979.
Hofstadter, D. R., and Dennett, D. C. *The Mind's I.* New York: Basic Books, 1981.
King, N. "Play: The Kindergartener's Perspective." *The Elementary School Journal,* 1979, *80* (2), 81–87.
Kuhn, T. S. *The Structure of Scientific Revolutions.* Chicago: University of Chicago Press, 1962.
McLoyd, V. C. "Social Class Differences in Sociodramatic Play: A Critical Review." *Developmental Review,* 1982, *2,* 1–30.
Manicas, P. T., and Secord, P. F. "Implications for Psychology of the New Philosophy of Science." *American Psychologist,* 1983, *38* (4), 399–413.
Morowitz, H. J. "Rediscovering the Mind." *Psychology Today,* 1980, *14* (3), 12–18.
Piaget, J. *Play, Dreams, and Imitation in Childhood.* New York: Norton, 1962 [1945].
Polanyi, M. *Science, Faith, and Society.* Chicago: University of Chicago Press, 1948.
Schank, R., and Abelson, R. "Scripts, Plans, and Knowledge." In P. Johnson-Laird and P. Wason (Eds.), *Thinking: Readings in Cognitive Science.* New York: Cambridge University Press, 1977.
Schwartzman, H. B. *Transformations: The Anthropology of Children's Play.* New York: Plenum, 1978.
Sutton-Smith, B., Botvin, G., and Mahoney, D. "Developmental Structures in Fantasy Narratives." Paper presented at the annual meeting of the American Psychological Association, Chicago, September 1978.
Watson, M. W., and Fischer, K. W. "Development of Social Roles in Elicited and Spontaneous Behavior During the Preschool Years." *Developmental Psychology,* 1980, *16* (5), 483–494.

Greta Fein is professor of education at the University of Maryland. She received her doctorate from Yale University in 1969 and is author of many articles and books on play and early education.

Some of the literature on this topic is reviewed.

Annotated Bibliography

Artin Göncü
Frank Kessel

Bateson, G. "A Theory of Play and Fantasy." *Psychiatric Research Reports,* 1955, 2, 39–51.

    This article presents Bateson's ideas on play-as-communication in a summary form. Based on his theory of metacommunication, Bateson illustrates the roles of messages about play in creation of play context. Although brief, this source is quite complicated for a beginning reader. *Steps to an Ecology of Mind* by the same author and *Transformations: The Anthropology of Children's Play* by Schwartzman provide detailed accounts of Bateson's view. [1]

Burke, K. *A Grammar of Motives.* Los Angeles: University of California Press, 1969.

    This is a basic source for the formulation of the dramatistic perspective as a technique for analyzing interaction. Chapter One, in which Burke introduces the notion of *dramatism* and defines its key terms, is most relevant for those who seek to apply dramatistic analysis to children's interactions. Though this original source is somewhat diffi-

---

    This bibliography has been drawn from suggestions made by the chapter authors. The number in brackets following each entry refers to the chapter, and hence author(s), in question.

cult for the beginning student, it is invaluable for those who seek to understand the foundations of dramatistic analysis. [2]

Franklin, M. B. "Play as the Creation of Imaginary Situations: The Role of Language." In S. Wapner and B. Kaplan (Eds.), *Toward a Holistic Developmental Psychology*. Hillsdale, N.J.: Erlbaum, 1983.

This chapter presents Franklin's discussion of children's play from a perspective which is consistent with a genetic dramatistic analysis. It focuses on the pragmatic rather than the thematic aspects of children's play interaction, and thereby on the conception of structure in playful social interaction. [2]

Gergen, K. *Toward Transformation in Social Knowledge*. New York: Springer-Verlag, 1982.

This book has the virtue of being written by an established social psychologist, of being up to date, and of comprehending the interpretive philosophical literature in ways relevant to psychology. His applications are to social and developmental psychology in particular. His metaphor is contextualist and he sees us in a constant and ongoing process of interpretation and reinterpretation of what we mean by psychology and what we mean by science. There is no final appeal to empiricism, and no way out. [4]

Glassie, H. *Passing the Time in Ballymenone*. Philadelphia: University of Pennsylvania Press, 1982.

This is a study of the culture and history of an Ulster community. Using the synthetic power of his discipline, folklore, Glassie addresses problems within a multiplicity of other disciplines such as anthropology, history, linguistics, archaeology, geography, art history, and literary history. In keeping with his enterprise — to write a historical ethnography of Ballymenone — Glassie spent seven years observing and participating in the lives of the people of this community.

For those of us concerned with understanding the meaning of texts, whether it be in relation to the world of childhood or adulthood, Glassie's work is a tour de force that illustrates how text is utterly implicated in context and can only be understood as part of a user-constructed system. [3]

Kaplan, B. "Genetic Dramatism: Old Wine in New Bottles." In S. Wapner and B. Kaplan (Eds.), *Toward a Holistic Developmental Psychology*. Hillsdale, N.J.: Erlbaum, 1983.

This chapter details how the dramatistic theory of Burke can be usefully applied to a developmental analysis of human interaction. With Burke's original writings, it forms a cornerstone of dramatistic analysis applied to children's social interaction. [2]

Manicas, P. T., and Secord, P. F. "Implications for Psychology of the New Philosophy of Science." *American Psychologist,* 1983, *38* (4), 399–413.

This article is a recent contribution to philosophy of science. Manicas and Secord present a concise account of the standard and Kuhnian view of science as well as the implications of the realist view. Manicas and Secord argue the need for situational, biographical, and historical information in psychological research. [5]

"Metaphors in the History of Psychology." An American Psychological Association Symposium at Anaheim, California, in 1983, with participants David Leary, Howard Gruber, Laurence Smith, and Karl H. Pribram.

Four excellent papers on the subtle ways in which many traditional assumptions in recent psychology are underlaid by metaphor. Pribram's discussion of the telecommunications and information measurement metaphors of Shannon and Weaver; the thermostat, feedback, and cybernetic control metaphors of Wiener; the wide range of metaphors based upon computer technology and programming, and the various hologram and pattern analysis metaphors was particularly illuminating. Pribram argued that such analogical reasoning is central to the future of science. [4]

Olson, D. R. (Ed.). *The Social Foundations of Language and Thought.* New York: Norton, 1980.

This book presents an excellent collection of studies on development of intentionality in dialogues. Various articles examine, in different ways and at different levels, how children carry on dialogues with one another and with adults. For a dynamic analysis of conversation, refer to the chapters by Brown and Kaye and Charney. [1]

Pepper, S. *World Hypotheses.* Berkeley: University of California Press, 1961.

Pepper states the irrepressible case for all of our thinking being analogical at root. He traces the history of formism, mechanism, contextualism, and organicism in philosophy and shows how, without difficulty, one can apply them to psychology. We are always interpreting; nature is not simply there. [4]

Polanyi, M. *Science, Faith and Society.* Chicago: University of Chicago Press, 1948.

Polanyi illustrates the personal and sociological dimensions of science in this book. Arguing against attempts to institutionalize scientific inquiry, Polanyi shows that science is indeed an expression and product of common faith. Attempts to eliminate or hide such faith are attempts to eliminate science. [5]

Rogoff, B. "Integrating Context and Cognitive Development." In M. E. Lamb and A. L. Brown (Eds.), *Advances in Developmental Psychology*, Vol. 2. Hillsdale, N.Y.: Erlbaum, 1982.

In this chapter, Rogoff argues that child development can best be understood within its social context. Drawing from Vygotsky and Gibson, Rogoff claims that context is not something external to children but is a dynamic process gaining meaning in interaction. [1]

Schutz, A. *On Phenomenology and Social Relations.* Chicago: University of Chicago Press, 1970.

This collection of essays offers a representation of Schutz's thoughts. In accordance with phenomenological theory, Schutz argues that each individual constructs his own world. He suggests that even the most socially stereotyped cultural ideas only exist in the minds of individuals who absorb them, interpret them on the basis of their own life situation, and give them a personal tinge. Within such a view of human interpretation and meaning, context is a dynamic and emergent notion which is more in the mind of the individual and his own stock of knowledge than in the surrounding physical environment. [3]

Artin Göncü is a research associate at the Center for Advancement of Child Care and Education and a lead teacher at the Human Development Laboratory, University of Houston. He received his Ph.D. from the University of Houston in 1983.

Frank Kessel is associate professor of psychology at the University of Houston. He received his Ph.D. from the University of Minnesota in 1969 and is coeditor of and contributor to The Child and Other Cultural Inventions.

Index

A

Abelson, R., 34, 35, 74, 75, 84
Acceptance statements, in play utterances, 10, 15
Action. *See* Behavior
American Educational Research Association (AERA), 1
Anchored episodes, in fantasy play, 30, 31, 33

B

Bamberg, M., 56, 69
Bateson, G., 6, 7, 8, 10, 20, 37, 39, 51, 56, 57, 58, 60, 69, 85
Behavior, in fantasy play, 29, 31, 32, 33, 34
Berlyne, D., 6, 60
Berndt, R., 8, 21
Bernstein, R. J., 53, 69
Botvin, G., 84
Bromley, D. B., 33, 35
Bronfenbrenner, U., 83, 84
Brown, R., 11, 20, 87
Bruner, J. S., 7, 11-12, 19, 20, 60
Burke, K., 27, 28, 29, 35, 46-47, 51, 57, 65, 69, 76, 78, 84, 85-86, 87

C

Character, in fantasy play, 29, 31, 32, 33, 34
Charney, R., 12, 13, 18, 21, 87
Children: at twenty-six months, 12; at thirty months, 12; at three years, 8-10, 12-13, 15-18; at four years, 8-9, 12-13, 76; at four-and-a-half years, 9-10, 14-18; at five years, 8-9, 12-13, 28-35, 78; at six years, 13, 78; at seven years, 28-35, 29-50, 78
Comeaux, D., 3n
Communication: asymmetry in, 12; play as, 7-9
Conrad, R., 9, 20
Content, context distinct from, 23-24. *See also* Text

Context: concept of, 37-39, 54; content distinct from, 23-24; to Forbes and Yablick, 57-58; to Göncü and Kessel, 56-57; in interpretive science, 55-56; issues related to, 73-79; to Kelly-Byrne, 58-59; in natural science, 54-55; as temporal or concurrent relationships, 74; and text in imaginative play, 53-70; and text in relationships, 37-51; as verbal behavior, 77-78
Conversation: discussion of findings on, 18-20; illustration of, 14-15; maintaining imaginative, 13-15; and metacommunication, 20; play as, 11-13; and social-cognitive development, 18; study of, 15-18
Corsaro, W., 56, 69

D

Damon, W., 1
Darwin, C., 73, 84
Dennett, D. C., 82, 83, 84
DeStefano, L., 6, 21
DeVries, R., 5n
Dewey, J., 3
Dickey, R., 5n
Dilthey, W., 53
Dore, J., 12, 20
Dramatism, in fantasy play, 26-28
Dramatistic pentad, 27
Dramatic content, organization of, 23-36

E

Einstein, A., 82
Elder, J. L., 6, 20, 21
Enslein, J., 21
Erikson, E. H., 6, 60, 73, 84
Ervin-Tripp, S., 12, 20

F

Fabling: concept of, 40; in relationships, 37-51
Fagen, R., 66, 69

91

Fantasy play: analysis of dramatic content in, 23–36; anchored episodes in, 30, 31, 33; coding for, 28–30; discussion of, 33–35; dramatic cohesion in, 30; dramatism in, 26–28; findings on, 30–33; methods of studying, 28–30; ratio in, 27, 29–30, 32–33, 35; reality-creation paradigm in, 25–26; transformational activities of, 25–26; and world building, 24–28
Fein, G. G., 5, 6, 20–21, 51, 71–84
Fenson, L., 76, 84
Field, T., 6, 21
Fischer, K. W., 72, 84
Folklore, and play, 61–62, 68–69
Forbes, D., 23–36, 57–58, 69, 73, 74, 75–76, 77, 79
Framing, in fantasy play, 24
Frank, L. K., 84
Franklin, M. B., 25, 26, 35, 86
Freud, S., 58, 60, 64–65, 71

G

Gadamer, H. G., 53, 59, 65, 69
Garvey, C., 8, 12, 21, 24, 27–28, 35, 77, 84
Geertz, C., 2, 3, 39, 51, 65, 66, 69, 81, 84
Gelman, R., 50, 51
Genishi, C., 76, 84
Gergen, K., 86
Gibson's research, 88
Glassie, H., 38, 50, 51, 86
Goffman, E., 24, 27, 35, 39, 49, 51, 65–66, 70
Goldenson, R. M., 84
Göncü, A., 1–3, 5–22, 56–57, 69, 72, 73, 74, 75, 77, 78–79, 84, 85–89
Gould, R., 73, 84
Groos's theory, 60
Gruber, H., 87

H

Hall, E., 54, 70
Halliday, M. A. K., 30, 35
Hans, J. S., 65, 70
Hartley, R. E., 73, 84
Harvard Graduate School of Education, 28
Hasan, R., 30, 35

Hawes, B., 61, 70
Heidegger, M., 53, 65, 70
Heraclitus, 64
Hofstadter, D. R., 80, 82, 83, 84
Homer, 64
Houston, University of, Human Development Laboratory at, 5n, 15
Hughes, L. A., 62, 70
Human development, and play, 67–68, 71–73
Husserl, E., 53
Hutt, C., 63, 69, 70

I

Imaginative behavior, concept of, 54
Interactions, symbolic nature of, 27
Interpretive science: context in, 55–56; and research on play, 64–66
Invitations, in play utterances, 9, 10

J

Jackowitz, E. R., 6, 21
Jones, B., 61, 70

K

Kant, I., 62
Kaplan, B., 27, 35, 86–87
Kaye, K., 12, 13, 18, 21, 87
Kelly-Byrne, D., 20, 37–51, 58–59, 60, 69, 70, 72, 73, 74, 75, 77, 78, 79
Kessel, F. S., 1–3, 5–22, 56–57, 69, 72, 73, 74, 75, 77, 78–79, 84, 85–89
Kessen, W., 2–3
King, N., 72, 84
Knapp, H., 61, 70
Knapp, M., 61, 70
Koewler, J. H., III, 6, 21
Köhler, W., 63, 70
Krasnor, L. R., 61, 62, 70
Kuhn, T. S., 79, 84, 87

L

Lamb, M., 68, 70
Leary, D., 87
Liberman's theory, 60
Livesly, W. O., 33, 35

M

McDowell, J., 61, 69, 70
McLoyd, V. C., 6, 16, 21, 77, 84

Mahoney, D., 84
Mands, conversational function of, 13, 15, 16, 17
Manicas, P. T., 81, 84, 87
Matthews, W. S., 21
Meacham, J. A., 2, 3
Mead, M., 71
Mink, L. O., 2, 3
Mitchell-Kernan, C., 12, 20
Moorin, E. R., 21
Morowitz, H. J., 82, 83, 84

N

National Institute of Mental Health, 23n
National Science Foundation, 23n
Natural science: context in, 54-55; and irrational events, 79-83; play as viewed by, 71-84; research on play by, 59-64
Negations, in play utterances, 10, 15
Nelson, K., 2, 3
Nietzsche, F., 64, 65, 66, 70

O

Object, in fantasy play, 29, 32
Object statements, in play utterances, 9, 10, 17, 18, 19
Olson, D. R., 13, 21, 87
Opie, I., 61, 70
Opie, P., 61, 70
Owens, T., 3n

P

Pederson, D. R., 6, 20, 21
Peevers, H., 33, 35
Pepler, D. J., 61, 62, 63, 70
Pepper, S., 87-88
Person perception, and fantasy play, 33-34
Piaget, J., 6, 7, 21, 50, 60, 71, 73, 84
Plans, in play utterances, 9, 10, 15, 17, 19
Plato, 60, 64, 65
Play: analysis of contextual-functional view of, 5-22; as-if concept of, 62; background on, 5-7; bibliography on, 85-89; classifying utterances in, 9-11; as communication, 7-9; conclusion on, 66-69; as conversation, 11-13; discussion of findings on, 18-20; fantasy, 23-36; and folklore, 61-62, 68-69; and human development, 67-68, 71-73; imaginative, 53-70; maintaining imaginative conversations in, 13-15; metacommunicative context of, 7-8; natural science view of, 71-84; as paradoxical framing, 39; and problem solving, 63; as reality, 64-65; research on, 59-66; as secondary, 60; settings for, 72-73; and socialization, 60-61; and society, 65-66; studies of, 5-7; text and context in, 53-70; theoretical viewpoints on, 6
Polanyi, M., 79, 80, 82, 84, 88
Pretense, and reality, 74-77
Pribram, K. H., 87
Purpose, in fantasy play, 29, 31, 32

Q

Quarton, C., 5n

R

Ramanadhan, R., 5n
Ramsay, D. S., 76, 84
Ratio: in fantasy play, 27, 29-30, 32-33, 35; and pretense and reality, 76
Reality, and pretense, 74-77
Reality-creation paradigm, in fantasy play, 25-26
Relationship: analysis of fabling in, 37-51; conclusion on, 50-51; discussion of, 42-50; session one in, 40-42, 44-45; session two in, 45-48; session three in, 48-50; study of, 39-42; temporal or concurrent, 74; tests in, 43-44; text and context in, 37-51
Responses, conversational function of, 13, 15, 16, 17
Rogoff, B., 19-20, 21, 88
Rook-Green, A., 21
Rorty, R., 2, 3
Rubin, K., 5, 6, 21, 50, 51, 63, 70

S

Scene, in fantasy play, 29, 31, 32, 33, 34
Schank, R., 34, 35, 74, 75, 84
Schiller, R. von, 62

Schutz, A., 48, 51, 53, 88
Schwartzman, H. B., 8, 9, 21, 23, 35, 49, 51, 75, 81, 84, 85
Secord, P. F., 33, 35, 81, 84, 87
Settings, for play, 72–73
Shannon's metaphors, 87
Sheldon, J., 5n
Singer's theory, 60
Situation, concept of, 38
Sluckin, A., 61, 70
Smith, L., 87
Spariosu, M., 60, 62, 64, 70
Spencer, H., 60
Spradley, J. P., 39, 51
Sutton-Smith, B., 6, 8, 19, 21, 39, 51, 53–70, 77, 79, 81, 82, 84

T

Termination statements, in play utterances, 10
Text: concept of, 53–54; and context in imaginative play, 53–70; and context in relationships, 37–51; as representation or presentation, 78–79
Torrance, N., 13, 21
Transformations, in play utterances, 9–10, 15, 17, 19

Turnabouts, conversational function of, 13, 15, 16, 17, 18
Turner, V., 39, 45, 51, 65, 66, 70

U

Unlinked utterances, conversational function of, 14, 15, 16, 17
Utterances, classifying, 9–11

V

Vandenberg, B., 21, 51
van Gennep, A., 45, 51
Van Hoorn, J., 1
Vygotsky, L. S., 6, 19, 21, 71, 88

W

Watson, M. W., 6, 21, 72, 84
Weaver's metaphors, 87
Wertsch, J. V., 2, 3
Whyte, W. F., 62, 70
Wiener, N., 87
World building, and fantasy play, 24–28

Y

Yablick, G., 23–36, 57–58, 69, 73, 74, 75–76, 77, 79